Bush Theatre

The Bush Theatre presents the world premiere of

The Invisible

by Rebecca Lenkiewicz

3 July–15 August 2015
Bush Theatre, London

The Invisible is kindly sponsored by The Law Society

The Invisible

by Rebecca Lenkiewicz

Cast (in order of appearance)

Gail	**Alexandra Gilbreath**
Ken	**Nicholas Bailey**
Riz / Ryan	**Scott Karim**
Aisha / Laura / Waitress	**Sirine Saba**
Shaun / Andy	**Niall Buggy**

Creative Team

Playwright	**Rebecca Lenkiewicz**
Director	**Michael Oakley**
Designer	**Ruth Sutcliffe**
Lighting Designer	**Richard Howell**
Sound Designer	**Ed Clarke**
Assistant Designer	**Nina Patel-Grainger**
Movement Director	**Etta Murfitt**
Company Stage Manager	**Kate Schofield**
Assistant Stage Manager	**Naomi Lee**
Production Electrician	**Nic Farman**

Rebecca Lenkiewicz and the Bush Theatre would like to thank:

Catherine Baksi, Saj Chaudhury, Lesley Emery, Andrew Hillier, Steve Hynes and all at Legal Action Group, Sue James, Caitriona McLaughlin, Richard Miller and all at The Law Society, Lucy Scott-Moncrieff, Meena Patel, Diane Sechi and Jenny Stokes.

Cast and Crew

Alexandra Gilbreath (Gail)

Alexandra is an Olivier Award-nominated actor whose theatre credits include *Shakespeare's Birthday Bash, The Merry Wives of Windsor* (both RSC), *Playhouse Creatures* (Chichester Festival Theatre), *Shallow Slumber* (Soho Theatre), *Othello* (Sheffield Crucible Theatre), *The Village Bike* (Royal Court Theatre), *Hay Fever* (Rose Theatre Kingston), *Twelfth Night* (RSC Stratford/ West End), *Lucky You* (Magic Key Productions), *Merry Wives: The Musical, The Tamer Tamed, The Taming of the Shrew, As You Like It, Romeo and Juliet, The Winter's Tale, Ghosts, Love's Labour's Lost* and *The Country Wife* (all RSC), *Cyrano De Bergerac* (RSC/ West End), *The House of Bernarda Alba* (Gate Theatre), *Hedda Gabler* (Ian Charleson Award, English Touring Co./ Donmar) and *King Lear* (West Yorkshire Playhouse). Television credits include *Father Brown, Casualty, WPC 56, Doctors, EastEnders* (all BBC), and *Midsummer Night's Dreaming* (RSC/ Google). Film credits include *A Hundred Streets, Tulip Fever, The All Together*, and *Dead Babies*. Alexandra is an associate artist with the RSC.

Nicholas Bailey (Ken)

Nicholas' theatre credits include *Macbeth* (Mercury Theatre), *Soho Streets* (Soho Theatre), *Breakfast with Mugabe* (Theatre Royal Bath), *Mela* (West Yorkshire Playhouse), *Become a Man* (Hackney Empire), *Blue on Blue* (Haymarket Basingstoke), *A Sense of Justice* (Perth Rep), *Mother Courage and Her Children* (Shared Experience), *Dreaming* (Manchester Royal Exchange, West End), *Life is a Dream* (Barbican/ Brooklyn Academy of Music), *Easy Access (For the Boys)* (Drill Hall), *Life is a Dream* (Edinburgh Royale Lyceum), *King Lear* (National Theatre), *Hamlet, The Winter's Tale* (both Manchester Library Theatre), and *Julius Caesar* (Manchester Royal Exchange). For television, Nicholas is best known for playing Dr Anthony Truman on *EastEnders*. Other credits include, *Siblings* (BBC3), *Doctors* (BBC), *Anubis House* (Lime Pictures, Nickelodeon), *Law & Order UK* (Kudos), *Miranda* (BBC), *Manchester Passion* (BBC4), *Walter Tull: Forgotten Hero, Inside Out* (BBC - presenter). Radio credits include *Tokolosh, Albion Towers, Midwich Cuckoos, The Archers* and *Silver Street* (BBC Radio).

Scott Karim (Riz / Ryan)

Scott's theatre credits include *The Merchant of Venice* (Globe Theatre), *Dara* (National Theatre), *Great Britain* (National Theatre/ Theatre Royal Haymarket), *Grand Budapest Hotel* (Secret Cinema), and *Othello* (National Theatre). For television he has appeared in *Holby City* (BBC).

Sirine Saba (Aisha / Laura / Waitress)

Sirine trained at RADA. Her theatre credits include *Fireworks, The Spiral* (Royal Court), *Holy Warriors, Anthony and Cleopatra* (Globe), *Next Fall* (Southwark Playhouse), *The Winter's Tale, Taming of the Shrew, Midsummer Night's Dream, Twelfth Night, HMS Pinafore* (Regent's Park Open Air), *The Keepers of Infinite Space* (Park), *The Fear of Breathing* (Finborough), *Scorched* (Old Vic Tunels), *Nation, Sparkleshark* (National Theatre), *Testing the Echo* (Out Of Joint/Tricycle), *Baghdad Wedding* (Soho), *Beauty and the Beast, Midnight's Children, The Tempest, The Winter's Tale, Pericles, Tales from Ovid, A Midsummer Night's Dream, A Warwickshire Testimony* (all RSC),

Cinderella (Bristol Old Vic), *House and Garden* (Northampton). Film and TV credits include *Lipstick*, *Exhibition*, *Maestro*, *Death of the Revolution*, *Doctors*, *I am Slave*, *Silent Witness*, *Footballer's Wives*, *The Bill* and *Prometheus*. Sirine has recorded a wide variety of plays, books and stories for BBC Radio 4 and BBC Radio 3.

Niall Buggy (Shaun / Andy)

Niall is an Oliver Award-winning actor whose best known roles include *Uncle Vanya* (Gate Theatre, Dublin and Lincoln Center, NYC), for which he won Best Actor in the Irish Times Theatre Awards, *Aristocrats* (Hampstead Theatre, Manhattan Theater Club) for which he won a number of awards including the Time Out Award, Obie Award in New York, Drama Desk Award and a Clarence Derwent Award. He was awarded the Olivier Award for Best Comedy Performance in *Dead Funny* and won the TMA Award for *Juno and the Paycock* (Wyndham's Theatre). Other theatre credits include *Penelope* (Druid Theatre, Edinburgh Festival, Hampstead Theatre), *Whistle in the Dark* (Kennedy Center), *The Gigli Concert* (Finborough Theatre), *A Kind of Alaska* (Gate Theatre), *The Hanging Gardens* (Abbey Theatre, Dublin), *The Importance of Being Ernest* (Harold Pinter Theatre), *Translations* (Sheffield Crucible), *Haunted* (Sydney Opera House and New York), *After Play* (Gate Theatre, Edinburgh and Sydney Festivals), and *Guys and Dolls* (Piccadilly Theatre). Television credits include *Inspector Lewis*, *Dalziel and Pascoe*, *Father Ted*, *The Bill* and *Once in a Lifetime*. Film credits include *Mamma Mia*, *Casanova*, *The Butcher Boy*, *Alien 3 The Playboys* and *Mr Turner*.

Rebecca Lenkiewicz (Playwright)

Rebecca is an award-winning writer who, in 2008, was the first living female playwright to have her work produced on the Olivier Stage at the National Theatre, London. Rebecca's screenplay *Ida*, co-written with Pawel Pawlikowksi, won Best Foreign Language Film awards at the 2015 Oscars, BAFTAs and Spirit Awards. Her plays have been performed at various theatres including the Arcola, the Soho, the Old Vic, the Almeida and on Broadway. Her next play *Jane Wenham: Witch of Walkern* is a touring production with Out of Joint (co-produced with the Arcola, Watford Palace and in association with Eastern Angles).

Michael Oakley (Director)

Michael is a winner of the prestigious JMK Award for Young Directors for which he directed *Edward II* at BAC. He was also Trainee Director in Residence at Chichester Festival Theatre and Co-Artistic Director of their pop-up venue Theatre on the Fly. Direction includes April De Angelis' adaptation of John Cleland's *The Life and Times of Fanny Hill* (Bristol Old Vic), the first revival of Terence Rattigan's *Variation On A Theme* (Finborough Theatre), *As You Like It* (OSC & Wilderness Festival), *Dido Queen of Carthage* (Marlowe Society, Cambridge), *Playhouse Creatures* (Chichester Festival Theatre), *The Changeling* (Southwark Playhouse), *Shooting Truth* (NT Connections) and *Graceland* (The 24 Hour Plays: Old Vic New Voices). Associate Direction includes *Taken at Midnight*, *Rosencrantz and Guildenstern Are Dead* (Chichester Festival Theatre and West End). *The Pajama Game (West End)*, *Relative Values* (Theatre Royal Bath and West End), *Kiss Me Kate* (The Old Vic) and *The King's Speech* (West End and UK tour). Assistant Direction includes *Inherit The Wind* (The Old Vic), *A Month in the*

Country, The Critic and *The Real Inspector Hound, Oklahoma!, Cyrano de Bergerac* (Chichester Festival Theatre), *tHe dYsFUnCKshOnalZ!* (Bush Theatre) and *Much Ado About Nothing* (Globe Education).

Ruth Sutcliffe (Designer)

Ruth's previous theatre credits include *The Taming of the Shrew* (RSC), *Hedda Gabler* (Royal & Derngate), *Kingdom of Earth* (The Print Room), *Yerma* (Gate Theatre and Hull Truck), *The Duchess of Malfi* (Theatre Royal Northampton), *Bronte* (Tricycle, and tour) and *The Boy on the Swing* (Arcola).

Richard Howell (Lighting Designer)

Richard's theatre credits include *Privacy* (Donmar Warehouse), *East is East* (Trafalgar Studios & UK Tour), *A Doll's House, Little Shop of Horrors* (Manchester Royal Exchange), *Cat on a Hot Tin Roof* (Northampton Royal, Northern Stage & Manchester Royal Exchange), *Playing for Time* (Sheffield Crucible), *Bad Jews* (Bath Ustinov, St James & Arts), *The Life and Time of Fanny Hill* (Bristol Old Vic), *Les Parents Terribles, The Dance of Death* (Donmar Trafalgar), *Utopia* (Soho Theatre/Newcastle Live), *The Recruiting Officer, Stepping Out* (Salisbury Playhouse), *The Island* (Young Vic), *Jack and the Beanstalk* (Lyric Hammersmith), *The Artist Man and the Mother Woman* (Traverse), *4000 Miles, Fifty Words* and *In A Garden* (Bath, Ustinov), *The Sound of Heavy Rain* (Paines Plough, Roundabout), *Arabian Nights* (Tricycle), *Romeo and Juliet* (York Theatre Royal and UK Tour), *Uncle Vanya, Snake in the Grass* (Print Room), *Sherlock's Last Case, Laurel and Hardy, The Tempest, Lettice and Lovage, Great Expectations, Heroes* and *Single Spies* (Watermill Theatre). Opera and Dance includes *Il Trittico, Flight, Madame Butterfly, La Fanciulla* (Opera Holland Park) *My First Cinderella, My First Coppelia* (English National Ballet) *Marriage of Figaro, La Clemenza Di Tito* (Royal Conservatoire, Glasgow) and *The Magic Flute* (Royal College of Music).

Ed Clarke (Sound Designer)

Ed has previously worked at the Bush Theatre on *The Royale, Perseverance Drive* and *Fear*. His other theatre credits include *The Infidel* (Theatre Royal Stratford East), *The Realness and Politrix* (The Big House), *Beauty and the Beast* (Young Vic), Danny Boyle's *Frankenstein* (National Theatre – Olivier Award nomination 2012), *Backbeat* (Duke of York's Theatre), *The Mysteries* and *The Good Hope* (National Theatre), *The Railway Children* (Waterloo International Station and Roundhouse Theatre Toronto – Olivier Award nomination 2011), *Fatal Attraction* (Theatre Royal Haymarket), *Backbeat* (Duke of York's), *Phoenix* and *Babylon* (BigHouse Theatre), *1 hour 18 minutes* (Sputnik Theatre), *His Teeth* (Only Connect Theatre), *The Wiz* (Birmingham Rep and West Yorkshire Playhouse), *Baby Doll* (Albery Theatre), *Alex* (Arts Theatre, UK and international tour), *Happy Now?* (Hull Truck Theatre), *Old Times* and *A Doll's House* (Donmar Warehouse), *Bad Man Christmas* (HMP Wormwood Scrubs), *The Wizard of Oz* and *Sandi Toksvig's Christmas Cracker* (Royal Festival Hall), *Singular Sensations* (Haymarket Theatre), *Twelfth Night* and *A Slice of Saturday Night* (Queen's Theatre Hornchurch), *The Milk Train Doesn't Stop Here Anymore, Treasure Island, The Cabinet of Doctor Caligari, Kindertoten-lieder, Then Again, Angela Carter's Cinderella, Cause Célèbre, Mrs Warren's Profession* and *A Midsummer Night's Dream* (Lyric Hammersmith), *Moti Roti Puttli Chunni, Running Dream* and Mike Leigh's *It's a Great Big Shame!* (Theatre Royal Stratford East).

Bush Theatre

We make theatre for London. Now.

The Bush is a world-famous home for new plays and an internationally renowned champion of playwrights. We discover, nurture and produce the best new writers from the widest range of backgrounds from our home in a distinctive corner of west London.

The Bush has won over 100 awards and developed an enviable reputation for touring its acclaimed productions nationally and internationally.

We are excited by exceptional new voices, stories and perspectives – particularly those with contemporary bite which reflect the vibrancy of British culture now.

Now located in a recently renovated library building on the Uxbridge Road in the heart of Shepherd's Bush, the theatre houses a 144-seat auditorium, rehearsal rooms and a lively café bar.

bushtheatre.co.uk

PASSMORE EDWARDS
PUBLIC
LIBRARY
"A powerhouse of new writing"
– Sunday Times Culture

Bush Theatre

Artistic Director	**Madani Younis**
Executive Director	**Jon Gilchrist**
Development Director	**Melanie Aram**
Events Manager	**Nathalie Bristow**
Café Bar Supervisor	**Charlie Buchan**
Community Producer	**Amanda Castro**
Café Bar Manager	**Ros Chirdaris**
Marketing Manager	**Lauren Clancy**
Press Representative	**The Corner Shop PR**
Literary Administrator	**Amy Davies Dolamore**
Associate Dramaturg	**Rob Drummer**
Associate Director	**Omar Elerian**
Production Manager	**Jessica Harwood**
Box Office Supervisor	**Farrar Hornby**
Development Manager	**Georgina Landau**
Technician	**William Lewis**
Administrator	**Carla Morris**
Finance Manager	**Candida Ronald**
General Manager	**Deborah Sawyerr**
Marketing and Digital Officer	**Leonie Sheridan**
Technician	**Aubrey Turner**
Development Officer (Trusts)	**Ine Van Riet**
Producer	**Sophie Watson**
Front of House Manager	**Matt Whayman**

Apprentices, Interns and Fellows
Lauren Bevan, Desara Bosnja, Natalie Garces-Bovett, Phoebe Walker

Duty Managers
Michael Kitchin, Eljai Morais, Shantanna Tabrizi

Front of House
Benedict Adeyemi, Lucy Atkinson, Lucy Avison, Pepter Buyungo, Charlotte Clark, Thomas Dennis, Melissa Dunne, Sophie Figon, Anna Griffiths, Luke Kemp, Andrew Lambe, Fred Lintern, Katie McHardy, James McLoughlin, Kate Morrison-Wynne, George Mulryan, Elissavet Ntoulia, Sarah-Jane Roberts, Remi Bruno-Smith, Rosie Spivey, Robert Wilson, James Thorpe-Woods, Rob Thorpe-Woods.

Board of Trustees
Simon Johnson (Chair), Gianni Alen-Buckley, Matthew Byam Shaw, Grace Chan, Stephen Greenhalgh, Khafi Kareem, Isabella Macpherson, David Parkhill, Nick Starr

Bush Theatre, 7 Uxbridge Road, London W12 8LJ
Box Office: 020 8743 5050 Administration: 020 8743 3584
Email: info@bushtheatre.co.uk

The Alternative Theatre Company Ltd (The Bush Theatre)
is a Registered Charity and a company limited by guarantee.
Registered in England no. 1221968. Charity no. 270080

THANK YOU
TO OUR SUPPORTERS

The Bush Theatre would like to extend a very special Thank You to the following Star Supporters, Corporate Members and Trusts & Foundations whose valuable contributions help us to nurture, develop and present some of the brightest new literary stars and theatre artists.

LONE STAR

Eric Abraham
Gianni Alen-Buckley
Michael Alen-Buckley
Rafael & Anne-Helene Biosse Duplan
Garvin & Steffanie Brown
Siri & Rob Cope
Alice Findlay
Aditya Mittal
Miles Morland
Lady Susie Sainsbury
James & Virginia Turnbull
Mr & Mrs Anthony Whyatt

HANDFUL OF STARS

Anonymous
Clive and Helena Butler
Clare Clark
Clyde Cooper
Simon & Katherine Johnson
Emmie Jones
Paul & Cathy Kafka
V & F Lukey
Charlie & Polly McAndrew
Paige Nelson
Philip & Biddy Percival
Robert Rooney
Joana & Henrik Schliemann
Philippa Seal & Philip Jones QC
The Van Tulleken Family
Charlotte & Simon Warshaw

RISING STARS

ACT IV
Nicholas Alt
Anonymous
Melanie Aram
Tessa Bamford
Charlie Bigham
David Brooks
Maggie Burrows
Simon Burstein
Matthew Byam Shaw
Benedetta Cassinelli
Tim & Andrea Clark
Sarah Clarke
Claude & Susie Cochin de Billy
Carole & Neville Conrad
Susie Cuff
Matthew Cushen
Liz & Simon Dingemans
Andrew & Amanda Duncan
Charles Emmerson

RISING STARS CONTINUED

Catherine Faulks
Lady Antonia Fraser
Rosie & Richard Gledhill
Global Cause Consultancy
Jack Gordon & Kate Lacy
Richard Gordon
Hugh & Sarah Grootenhuis
Thea Guest
Lesley Hill & Russ Shaw
Madeleine Hodgkin
Bea Hollond
Caroline Howlett
Ann & Ravi Joseph
Davina & Malcolm Judelson
Kristen Kennish
Nicola Kerr
Sue Knox
Isabella Macpherson
Penny Marland
Michael McCoy
Judith Mellor
Caro Millington
David Mills
Ann Montier
Georgia Oetker
Mark & Anne Paterson
Lauren Prakke
Barbara Prideaux
Emily Reeve
Renske & Marion
Sarah Richards
John Seal and Karen Scofield
Jon & NoraLee Sedmak
John & Tita Shakeshaft
Diane Sheridan
Saleem & Alexandra Siddiqi
Melanie Slimmon
Brian Smith
Nick Starr
Ed Vaizey
Marina Vaizey
Francois & Arrelle von Hurter
Trish Wadley
Amanda Waggott
Sir Robert & Lady Wilson
Peter Wilson-Smith & Kat Callo
Alison Winter
Andrew & Carey Wright

CORPORATE MEMBERS

LEADING LIGHT

Winton Capital Management

LIGHTBULB

The Agency (London) Ltd

SPONSORS & SUPPORTERS

Drama Centre London
Kudos Film & TV
MAC Cosmetics
Markson Pianos
Finlay Brewer
The Groucho Club
The Law Society
Ideas Tap
Waitrose Community Matters
West 12 Shopping & Leisure Centre

TRUSTS AND FOUNDATIONS

The Andrew Lloyd Webber Foundation
The Austin and Hope Pilkington Trust
BBC Performing Arts Fund
The City Bridge Trust
Coutts Charitable Trust
The Daisy Trust
The D'Oyly Carte Charitable Trust
EC&O Venues Charitable Trust
Foundation for Sport and the Arts
Garfield Weston Foundation
Garrick Charitable Trust
The Gatsby Charitable Foundation
The Goldsmiths' Company
Hammersmith United Charities
The Harold Hyam Wingate Foundation
The Idlewild Trust
Japan Foundation
Jerwood Charitable Foundation
John Lyon's Charity
The J Paul Getty Jnr Charitable Trust
The John Thaw Foundation
The Laurie & Gillian Marsh Charitable Trust
The Leverhulme Trust
The Martin Bowley Charitable Trust
Royal Victoria Hall Foundation
Sir Siegmund Warburg's Voluntary Settlement
Sita Trust
The Theatres Trust
The Thistle Trust
The Williams Charitable Trust
The Worshipful Company of Grocers

If you are interested in finding out how to be involved, please visit the 'Support Us' section of www.bushtheatre.co.uk, email development@bushtheatre.co.uk or call 020 8743 3584

PUBLIC FUNDING

Thank you to
The 144 Club

In 2014 we launched the 144 Club to help us grow a play at the Bush Theatre. Just 144 members (one for every seat in our theatre) directly support one show a year through development, rehearsal and production. This year members of the 144 Club have supported *The Invisible* and for that we give our heartfelt thanks.

144 Club Members are:

Anonymous
Daniel Abell
Moira Armstrong
Annabel Baring
Rosalind Benstead
Vanessa Brown
Catharine Browne
Jordi Castillo
Peter S Chapman
Jane Collins
Clyde Cooper
Elizabeth Cox
Defibrillator Theatre
Pat Devito-French
Mike Dickson
Meg Dobson
Patricia Dolphin
Lesley Emery
Stuart Ffoulkes
Susan Fletcher
Colin Harris
David Harrison
Nicola Kerr
Janice Ketley
Georgina Landau
Kirsty Lang
Patrick Leslie
Gavin Maclean
Kasia Markham
Miranda & David Moody
Toby Moorcroft
John Murphy
Tess Nowell
Joanna Prior
Ren Ruszkiewicz
Tony Saville Sneath
Barry Serjent
Susie Simkins
Paula Sinclair
Bridget & Rob Somekh
Janie Spring
Mark Stearman
Karen Stobart
Gillian Thorpe
Rachel Tyson
The van Tulleken Family
Zoe Weldon

The Invisible

Are you invisible? Of course not. Who could be invisible these days with the pervasiveness of social media and the escalation of surveillance?

As fully functioning members of society with wide-ranging interests and reasonably active social lives we're operating day to day with demands placed upon us that are generally offset by the brief relief of weekends and occasional treats, like a trip to the theatre.

A play that focuses upon our justice system is unusual, noteworthy, even curious. But surely the issues that it might raise will not affect us personally? Or could they?

Nobody expects their partner to walk out on them, to lose their job unfairly, to have a life-changing accident or illness that deprives them of their ability to earn a living. But what if you or someone from your family has the misfortune to be involved such a situation?

The matters that were traditionally covered by this country's Legal Aid scheme included complex, life-changing issues such as family breakdown, homelessness, and employment. However, the Legal Aid, Sentencing and Punishment of Offenders Act 2012 (LASPO) removed a host of areas from the scope of the scheme.

Legal Aid is no longer available in most clinical negligence cases, employment matters, private law family cases (other than where there is domestic violence, child abuse or child abduction), many housing law cases, debt cases, immigration matters, in the area of education and welfare law. Further, LASPO also altered the initial requirements that must be fulfilled before a citizen can receive assistance in respect of those matters that are still covered

Legal Aid may not have disappeared completely, but it has been very severely curtailed. For example, those victims of domestic abuse who need help in resolving disputes over money or their children must now provide 'prescribed evidence' indicating that they have suffered domestic violence within two years prior to an application for Legal Aid being submitted. Yet many victims of domestic violence do not have this 'prescribed evidence' – particularly if there has been psychological rather than physical abuse.

In 2014, a survey conducted by Rights of Women, Women's Aid and Welsh Women's Aid found that over half of the women that they spoke to who had suffered or were suffering as a result of an abusive partner did not have the evidence required to obtain Legal Aid. Victims were frequently too isolated or too frightened to speak out at the time.

So, what do you do if you have the misfortune to be involved in such difficult circumstances and do not have the money to instruct a lawyer privately? Frankly, you only have two options. The first is to represent yourself and endeavour to deal with often life-changing issues in busy courtrooms with unfamiliar and often very technical procedures. The second is to just walk away.

Legal Aid is not a welfare benefit. It is essential for a humane, just and civilised society. It ensures that the weak and the powerless – the invisible – receive justice, that most fundamental of rights.

There is no doubt that the changes brought in by LASPO have impacted on the ability of some of the most disadvantaged members of our society to defend and enforce their most fundamental rights. The situation needs to be urgently reviewed.

ANDREW CAPLEN

President, Law Society of England and Wales 2014/2015, July 2015

The Invisible

Rebecca Lenkiewicz's first play was *Soho – A Tale of Table Dancers* which won a Fringe First at Edinburgh and opened the Arcola Theatre in 2001. *The Night Season* opened at the National Theatre in 2004 and won the *Evening Standard* Most Promising Playwright Award. Other plays include *Her Naked Skin* at the Olivier Theatre, *The Painter* at the Arcola Theatre and *Shoreditch Madonna* at the Soho Theatre. Adaptations include Ibsen's *Ghosts* and *An Enemy of the People* at the Arcola and then at the Manhattan Theatre Club, Broadway. Rebecca has written many dramas and adaptations for BBC Radio including *Sarah and Ken* and *Ladder of Years*. With the film's director Pawel Pawlikowski she co-wrote *Ida*, which won the BAFTA for Best Film in 2015 and the Oscar for Best Foreign Film 2015.

also by Rebecca Lenkiewicz from Faber

REBECCA LENKIEWICZ: PLAYS ONE
(*The Night Season, Shoreditch Madonna, Her Naked Skin, The Painter*)

GHOSTS
AN ENEMY OF THE PEOPLE
(*after Ibsen*)

THE TURN OF THE SCREW
(*after Henry James*)

REBECCA LENKIEWICZ

The Invisible

ff

FABER & FABER

First published in 2015
by Faber and Faber Ltd
74–77 Great Russell Street
London WC1B 3DA

Typeset by Country Setting, Kingsdown, Kent CT14 8ES
Printed in England by CPI Group (UK) Ltd, Croydon CR0 4YY

All rights reserved
© Rebecca Lenkiewicz, 2015

The right of Rebecca Lenkiewicz to be identified as author
of this work has been asserted in accordance with Section 77
of the Copyright, Designs and Patents Act 1988

All rights whatsoever in this work are strictly reserved.
Applications for permission for any use whatsoever,
including performance rights, must be made in advance, prior to
any such proposed use, to Casarotto Ramsay and Associates Ltd,
Waverley House, 7–12 Noel Street, London W1F 8GQ.
No performance may be given unless a licence
has first been obtained.

*This book is sold subject to the condition that it shall not,
by way of trade or otherwise, be lent, resold, hired out
or otherwise circulated without the publisher's prior consent
in any form of binding or cover other than that in which
it is published and without a similar condition including
this condition being imposed on the subsequent purchaser*

A CIP record for this book
is available from the British Library

ISBN 978–0–571–32772–0

2 4 6 8 10 9 7 5 3 1

To all legal aid lawyers, past and present,
with respect and admiration

Acknowledgements

Rebecca Lenkiewicz would like to thank
Madani Younis, Rob Drummer, Dinah Wood,
Steve King, Mel Kenyon, Patrick Maggs,
Simon Trussler, everyone at the Bush Theatre
and the cast and company.

The Invisible was first performed at the Bush Theatre, London, on 3 July 2015. The cast, in order of appearance, was as follows:

Gail Alexandra Gilbreath
Ken Nicholas Bailey
Riz / Ryan Scott Karim
Aisha / Laura / Waitress Sirine Saba
Shaun / Andy Niall Buggy

Director Michael Oakley
Designer Ruth Sutcliffe
Lighting Designer Richard Howell
Sound Designer Ed Clarke

Characters

Gail
British, white, forties

Ken
British, black, forties.

Riz
Pakistani, thirties

Aisha
Pakistani, thirties

Laura
British, thirties

Shaun
Irish, sixties

Ryan
British Asian, thirties

Andy
British, white, sixties

Waitress
French, twenties

The play can be performed with
two female actors and three male actors,
doubling as follows:

Aisha / Laura / Waitress
Riz / Ryan
Shaun / Andy

THE INVISIBLE

The action is set in various locations
which do not have to be more than suggested.

When stage directions and/or dialogue
are set between rules, it denotes that
the action is imagined by one of the characters,
a brief dreamscape which might be subtly
supported with light or sound . . . or might not.

PROLOGUE

Recorded voices are heard. Some are from the 1960s television documentary Seven Up, *following the paths of children from age seven upwards.*

A privileged young boy talks about how he doesn't 'not like' the poor but doesn't want them to come to his school because they're dirty.

A working-class boy becomes a loner later in life and discusses his mental health.

A modern-day judge talks about access to justice. Snippets of humanity.

While these images are projected Shaun dances to his iPod. In separate spaces the people of the play inhabit their lives. Ken looks at photographs of his children. He blows into a paper bag to prevent a panic attack. Gail reads a surreal pile of files. Aisha sews a dress. Riz prays.

SCENE ONE

A pink restaurant. Night. Gail and Ken sit opposite each other at a dinner table. Gail has a glass of rosé. There are glasses of water on the table. They look through the menu. Ken has had a few drinks before arriving at the restaurant and is trying to sober up. Gail stops and puts both her feet firmly on the ground.

Gail Can you feel that?

Ken looks at her. Gail concentrates. She looks at him, he shakes his head. Gail bends towards the floor and puts one hand on the floor.

The vibrations. There must be an underground line here.

Ken nods. Gail sits back up again.

I think I'll have another glass of rosé. Shall we get a bottle?

Ken nods.

Will you have some?

Ken nods.

Okay. Good.

Ken shakes his head.

No? Okay. I can get through a bottle . . . if we're eating.

Ken Eating would be good.

Gail Actually I'm not sure . . . Maybe I'm not hungry.

Ken No?

Gail No . . . I'll have a drink and then I think I might go.

Ken You're going because . . . ?

Gail You were late. And you've had a few drinks.

Ken Two. Two pints. And a shot. She's bringing coffee. Okay?
I'm sorry. Stay. It'll be fun.

Gail I'll have another glass of wine.

Ken Exactly. Catch up.

Gail I didn't think it was a race.

Pause.

Ken Why are so many Indian restaurants pink?

Gail looks back at the menu.

In Denmark there's a TV show where two people meet for the first time and on the same day they get married.

Gail She's disappeared. I'm going to have a smoke.

Ken You won't come back.

Gail Yes, I will.

Ken Leave something here so you'll come back.

Gail What, like a shoe?

Ken Your purse.

Gail This isn't a hostage situation.

Ken No, it's a date. It's great.

Gail Do the couples get paid?

Ken Which couples?

Gail The ones on the show. Who meet and marry. Or do they just want to be on TV?

Ken No, they genuinely want a husband or wife. It's called *Marriage at First Sight*.

Beat.

Then they follow their progress.

Beat.

I had a Danish girlfriend. Divorce is very easy there. You can do it online.

Ken drinks some water. He pours some water on his hands and pats his face with it.

Ken Tell me about your work . . .

Gail It's my night off.

Ken Thank you.

Gail For what?

Ken For staying. What are you going to eat? Chicken?

Gail I'm a vegetarian.

Ken That's okay.

Gail I know it is.

Ken Fish?

Gail No.

Ken That's fine. A lot of vegetarians don't eat fish.

Gail Real vegetarians don't eat fish. Or meat. They don't eat it.

Ken But those fish oils. They'll keep you going. Your brain. Your knee joints. Depression. How can you do without them? You're okay. You look strong and healthy.

Gail Do you want to inspect my teeth?

Ken So . . . I'm just out of a car crash of a marriage . . . You work in a law centre, yeah? And you're . . . ?

Gail A vegetarian. I know. It's a lot to take in.

Ken I'm a good dancer. I bet you're a good dancer.

Gail I am.

Ken We should ask them to put some music on. Stop talking. Start dancing.

Gail and Ken get up and dance to a great Motown number for a few moments. They dance fantastically together. Then they sit back down.

Ken You don't have children?

Gail No. I've never had the time.

Ken See. We're doing okay. This is a pretty good level of talk. Don't you think? It's like a good marriage-level sort of conversation. Convivial.

Gail I've never been married.

Ken Impressive. I liked your write-up. You sounded very . . . optimistic.

Gail No. I'm not.

Ken You are. Compared to the people I know. You wrote about justice.

Gail Really? I must have had too much red wine before I filled it in.

A Waitress approaches with a cafetière of coffee. She puts it down with a cup.

Waitress Are you ready to order?

Ken A new head. A new body. And a new life, please. And Rachel would like a new soul mate.

Ken laughs.

Gail We might just stick with drinks.

Waitress You have to eat. Sorry. It's a legal thing.

Ken See? And you're a lawyer.

Gail Come back to us, yes?

Waitress Okay. We've got some specials there.

Ken Specials. Good. You should be in films, you know, not carrying trays around? Shouldn't she?

Gail What?

Ken Be in a film. Or modelling something. No?

Gail I'm going to have a fag.

The Waitress walks away.

Ken Have you always smoked?

Gail I wasn't born smoking, no. My name's Gail. Not Rachel.

Ken You lied to me.

Gail I didn't. I've never said my name was Rachel.

Ken When I came in I called you Rachel.

Gail Yes. And I let it go.

Ken Okay . . . Take two. Ken and Gail meet. How is it for you?

Gail This? Well . . . it's not great, Ken.

Ken Tell me about your cases.

Gail No. We're like doctors. Confidential.

Ken I'm not asking for names. Do you cover family law?

Gail No. I studied it. But we do mainly housing and immigration.

Ken Do you remember your studies?

Gail Vaguely. Do you?

Ken No. So what's the centre like?

Gail There's a lot of disappointment in one small building. A few successes too. Right . . . cigarettes.

She gets her cigarettes from her clutch bag.

Do you? Smoke?

Ken Me yes. I smoke . . . I drink . . . I vape . . . I chew Nicorette . . . I do dope . . . coke . . . Berocca . . . Red Bull . . . Smarties . . . I do everything. I'm terrible.

Gail Will you join me then?

Ken Let's order first. So you like it? The law?

Gail I'm probably addicted to it.

Ken The adrenalin?

Gail Hope. I've become expert at adjusting people's expectations. I can't stand that the law is seen as something foreign. It should be taught in schools. Your rights. Just like English and French is.

Ken So you don't get parents coming in? Families?

Gail No. What do you do?

Ken Nothing right now.

He pours some coffee.

Why did you go into law?

Gail I can't remember. What did you do then?

Ken Secret.

Gail You're not going to remember any of this tomorrow, are you?

Ken I will. Your face.

Gail No. I'm probably having a conversation with myself essentially.

Ken You're not. It's complicated, isn't it? The whole thing of . . . people.

Gail It's been a while.

Ken nods.

Ken Are you still capable of giving yourself to someone?

Gail Is that the transaction? It sounds pretty dramatic.

Ken Really? I think it sounds warm . . . comforting. Sexy.

Gail I've probably found myself lonelier with someone than I ever was by myself.

Ken Are you lonely now? Right now?

Gail . . . No.

Ken Good. Who do you like? What music do you like?

Gail You're drunk, Ken.

Ken nods.

Ken You'd know if I was really pissed. Who? Leonard Cohen.

Gail That was on my profile.

Ken laughs, Gail almost wants to laugh.

I saw an interview with him recently. They asked about women and he said something like 'People have very high expectations about love. But if you go into it all expecting torture then you might be pleasantly surprised.' And I thought that was pretty astute.

Ken Words. You like your words. And poets. Women like poets. Leonard Cohen. You responded to him. Why do women like poets?

Gail I don't think women like all poets. Men like poets too, don't they?

Ken Not so much. I mean, being a poet can actually swing it for someone, can't it? Why is that? Because a man can write something . . . lyrically . . . why would that guarantee anything beyond the fact that he could write something lyrically?

Gail That's the point. It's away from all things concrete. And writing a beautiful lyric, that might be enough.

Ken It's never enough. People never have enough.

Gail Do you like Leonard Cohen?

Ken He's okay. No, actually I don't.

Gail Why not?

Ken It doesn't matter.

Gail Go on. We won't see each other again.

Ken You've decided that, have you?

Gail Yes. See. I'm being honest. Why don't you like him?

Ken He's for people who want to pretend they're tortured.

Gail What absolute bollocks. Have you ever even listened to his lyrics? His music.

Ken That's sweet. You're defending him and you don't even know the man.

Gail I do know him. Through his work.

Ken I'm sorry. I was sort of joking anyway. Being . . . provocative.

Gail Right.

Ken You okay? Is this okay?

Gail I think I need to go.

Ken Because I pretended not to like Leonard Cohen?

Gail No because . . . because I'm exhausted. You were late and you're pissed and I want to be by myself. Sorry.

Ken No, I'm sorry.

Gail Right. I'm going.

Ken I was trying to make you laugh, that's all . . . Forgive me. I'm not at my best right now.

Gail You shouldn't be meeting strangers then.

Ken You're right . . . I have two children. One's at reception, the other's just started at the infants. I'm not with their mother. Obviously. Tell me about your work.

Gail No. You don't tell me what to talk about.

Ken You're angry with me.

Gail You tell me something.

Ken Okay . . . I've taken some time off at the moment. I sold medical instruments. And suddenly that didn't seem so important. So I sold infinite amounts of catheters. Glamorous. But actually giving people the right to pee comfortably . . . it's a big one. I had to sell up. I gave everything to my wife and kids. And now . . . I don't have a pot to piss in. Sorry.

Gail Your children need a home.

Ken They do.

Gail Money's not important.

Ken What is then?

Gail Freedom probably. Keeping your sense of humour.

Ken stops. He cannot respond.

Ken I'm in a bit of a state at the moment.

Gail Yes, I sort of gathered that.

Ken How are you? Are you in a state?

Gail Maybe. On a slightly different scale I suspect.

Ken What's your scale?

Gail We might be losing our premises. And if that happens I'll lose my job. And I've someone who works with me. I'm responsible for her. I'll have to let her go.

Ken Can't you just move somewhere else?

Gail No. We've been on a peppercorn sort of rent because our work was so community based. We can't afford to rent anywhere else.

Ken I'm sorry.

Gail That's all right. It's not your fault, is it?

Ken Nobody's fault.

Gail It is. It's the government.

Ken I'm not quite up to all of this. I'm suddenly incredibly tired.

Gail Okay . . . well, let's put this one down to experience, Ken. Go our separate ways.

Ken No. No we can't. The tiredness is gone. Seriously . . . You're beautiful, Gail.
There's a Gail . . . in *Carlito's Way*. My favourite film. Al Pacino.

Gail Shall we get the bill?

Ken Carlito he's come out of prison and Gail he's mad about her and she's working in a strip club. But he knocks down her door to give her some cheesecake . . . It's about redemption really. It's Al at his best. At the beginning. You see him being wheeled around half dead on a stretcher through Grand Central Station. All the blood is draining out of him. And I know how that feels. Having your colour drained out of you like that.

Gail Right.

Ken Gail . . . it's really important to me that you stay for dinner.

Gail It's not so important to me.

Ken I'm asking you . . . please. As one human being to another.

Gail And I'm saying no, Ken.

Ken That's what Gail says in the film. Exactly that. But he smashes the door down anyway.

Gail Look . . . we don't know each other.

Ken You must have liked my picture.

Gail It was all right. Just like mine was all right. It's all a bit of a lottery, isn't it?

Ken No, yours is beautiful. Kind. But you can't judge someone in less than ten minutes.

Gail I'm not judging. I'm just feeling . . . like going.

Ken No. I have a young son and daughter. I'm not allowed to see them.

Gail I'm sorry about that.

Ken I have no access to my children.

Gail That's harsh.

Ken And I love them. I love them as though someone shot me through with a shotgun. Now that I don't see them. Smell them. Hold them. I'm shattered, Gail.

Gail Right . . .

Ken On the way here I was all right. Feeling fine. Then I was on the tube, and I saw a mother with her son. And the kid stared at me . . . and he was listening to some tunes with her. A little boy. About four. One headphone in his ear, one in his mother's. Simple. And I lost it. Had to get out and cry like a kid. Had to have a few shots. I'm paper thin. You don't have children.

Gail No.

Ken You sway. It's like permanent jet lag. You lose all your confidence. Because your world has gone. You worry every minute that they think you don't care. That you've abandoned them. I snapped at Billy the day before I left and he'll think my going was connected to that. How are they supposed to understand it when you just disappear? There's a hole. Like someone died.

Gail You have rights. You must have looked into it?

Ken I did. But I'm broke. I can't afford a solicitor. I'm going to have to face Ellie in court. Myself.

Gail Ken. I'm going to leave now.

Ken I'm telling you this. We're here and now. You do all this work for refugees and you can't listen to someone who is sitting opposite you.

Gail That's my job.

Ken So you only do it because they pay you?

Gail I do it because I'm passionate about it. And I'm an expert at it. I've done it most of my life. And this is my one night off from trawling through pages about various cases which range from the domestic to the tragic. But I am going to go and do some reading. I hope it works out with your children.

She gets up to leave. Ken grabs her clutch bag which is on the table.

Ken Gail . . . don't.

Gail Don't tell me what to do! That's a mistake, Ken. Give me my bag.

Ken I need you.

Gail Shut up and give me my bag.

Ken I chose you!

Gail That is mine!

Ken Because you're a lawyer . . . because you could tell me how to go about it . . .

Gail What?

Ken I need your advice. I saw it in your profile. You enjoy helping people with advice. Solving problems, you said.

Gail You asked me out on a date for legal advice?

Ken Not like this. It wasn't meant to be like this. I didn't mean it to be drastic. Or to even tell you. I was just going to ask a few gentle . . . But then I broke down on the tube . . . and it's best to be honest, no? Just . . . I can't quite get on top of things. I just wanted a conversation about the ins and outs.

Gail Please give me my purse.

Ken I will. I'll pay the bill. I'm sorry. I'm so sorry. I didn't know what to do.

He gives the clutch bag to Gail. For some moments both their hands are on the bag. Gail takes it and Ken breaks down. Utterly. Gail hesitates. She walks out. Ken cries. Ken keeps crying. Gail comes back to him and sits down. He sees that she has come back. He tries to give her his hand.

Gail I don't want your hand. Don't touch me. Keep your hand. Get a hold of yourself and I'll talk you through the best procedures. Ten minutes of free legal advice. Then I'm gone. For ever.

Ken nods, tries to gather himself.

The longer you cry the less time you have. Pull yourself together. For fuck's sake . . . For your kids'. Now.

Ken gathers himself. Looks at Gail.

SCENE TWO

Pakistan. A room. Night. Aisha and Riz are alone whilst a party happens in the next room. They are excited. Aisha looks at a large map of London.

Aisha How long before your auntie comes in?

Riz Not long.

Aisha Are we being rude?

Riz No. We've been talking to everyone all evening. We deserve five minutes to ourselves.

Aisha Can we not have ten? Put your finger on Southall.

Riz does.

London's vast. Do you actually know how to get around the whole city?

Riz You don't need to know. It's like a series of villages. And you stay in your neighbourhood. Southall is our village.

Aisha I can't imagine your mother out there.

Riz She manages okay. She has a friend or two. But she likes it better here.

Aisha I always thought I'd end up in London. Why would I think that? Can we go to the Kew Gardens?

Riz Course we can. But it's expensive. You don't just walk in.

Aisha On my birthday then. You've inherited a business. We could probably adopt a tree or buy a greenhouse there.

Riz I've inherited twelve taxi cabs.

Aisha Your mother calls it a fleet of cars.

Riz It is not a fleet.

They laugh.

Aisha Your mother would prefer it if I was younger. Should we go back in?

Riz No. And she'll be fine once she has a grandchild.

Aisha Is she not fine now? At least you're getting married.

Riz She is. She's just waiting. It'll be good. A baby will take her attention away from me.

Aisha What does your mother do there? When you're at work?

Riz . . . She likes to cook. She keeps close to home mostly.

Aisha I'm going to do Business English.

Riz You won't need it.

Aisha Then I could help you with the cabs.

Riz You won't need business English for our office. It's very small.

Aisha Twelve cabs is good. Will I get one to use? Just for me?

Riz You might get a bicycle.

Aisha A bicycle? Even better.

Riz Get there. Acclimatise. Assimilate.

Aisha I never felt quite like I belonged here. I'll get some sort of job, shall I? They do, don't they? Do you think I should?

Riz You won't need one. You can keep Mum company. She's addicted to the soaps even though she doesn't understand them. It's the only thing that makes Mum laugh.

Aisha Don't you make her laugh? You're funny.

Riz No. She's pretty serious when it comes to me.

Aisha My family have bought presents for you all. They're not brilliant. But they tried.

Riz You could give me paper birds and I would be happy. Did you know we almost met at my aunt's wedding? When you were a girl.

Aisha Mum said. I remember that day. I had measles.

Riz I wish you'd been there.

Aisha I'm glad I wasn't. I was covered in red dots. And I looked like a boy. My hair didn't grow. You definitely wouldn't have chosen me for your future wife.

Riz Marriage will change everything. In a good way.

Aisha (*whispers*) Someone's outside. Listening?

Riz No.

Aisha and Riz listen. A noise of someone walking away.

Aisha There was someone.

Riz My auntie then. She needs to know everyone's business.

Aisha And she's your mother's sister?

Riz My father's.

Aisha I hope I won't drive you crazy with my questions.

Riz Questions are good. They are the only way to move forward. We need to know everything about each other. People are so much stronger together than apart.

Aisha They are. Mostly.

Riz When are they not?

Aisha Well, a mother is stronger as she has a different perspective once she's had a child. But she's weaker as she has everything to lose by losing the child.

Riz Why would she lose it?

Aisha Just if she did. The strongest person has no one to lose, I suppose.

Riz And no one to live for.

Aisha We all need that. Some people don't seem to need it. They're self-contained. They enjoy the distance.

Riz We should go back in . . . I want no distance from you. None at all. I want an invisible thread always between your hand and mine. To know where you are. What you're thinking.

He kisses Aisha's hand.

Aisha When I was young I loved the Spiderman cartoons. How he just leapt from building to building with his web. He went so fast. And he just kept escaping every situation.

'Superhero' music as Aisha becomes a touch ninja, dances with the memory of Spiderman and gives a kick.

Riz Why did you like it?

Aisha The way he leapt over the buildings. Through the alleys. See now. I am flying from here to there. I have become Spiderman.

Riz A crazy woman. I am marrying a crazy woman.

Aisha And we'll have a child. And he will be crazy too.

Riz You might have a daughter. A son for me and a daughter for you.

Riz and Aisha really look at each other, stopped. Riz kisses her, at first tentatively but it becomes passionate. They kiss each other more and then stop, slightly awkward.

Aisha I looked up the temperature. It's six degrees when you get there. Nine degrees by the time I join you in a month's time.

Riz It is cold.

Aisha I'll make it warmer when I get there. I will. I promise I will.

Riz It's grey over there. Very grey.

Aisha I'm going to get some Uniqlo jeans. They say they're the best cut and value. Have you seen Westfield?

Riz No.

Aisha There are two. One east, one west. Should I get some? What do you think?

Riz You do whatever you want. Or maybe ask Mother. She'll know what's best.

Aisha I will. I'll ask her about everything . . .
That was nice, Riz.

Riz What was?

Aisha Kissing you.

Riz My mother found my father, you know? When he was dead. You never mention him.

Aisha I'm sorry. I was leaving it to you.

Riz kisses Aisha's hand. He takes a moment to come back to her.

Riz I'll be a good father.

Aisha You will.

Riz My theory is that if you have bad parents you either become a terrible parent yourself or an excellent one. There is no middle ground. People repeat or they break the cycle and improve on the poverty they experienced. Emotionally. It's a decision. You'll be a great mother.

Aisha I've had an easier time than you. We'll both be good. And let's not hurry into it. Let's know each other . . . completely. Before we bring a little one into the world.

Riz I don't know what my mother would say to that.

Aisha It's not your mother's decision.

Riz I know. I'm a very lucky man.

Aisha You are. We're both very blessed.

Riz Blessed? I've never been blessed before.

Aisha You were. You just didn't know it.

Riz I wasn't, truly. But I am. Now.

Aisha And you like it?

Riz Very much. You're my angel.

Aisha I'm not an angel. I have terrible thoughts sometimes, Riz.

Riz Of what?

Aisha No matter. Later. When we are as one. We're blessed.

Riz kisses Aisha's forehead and Aisha leaves.
Riz prays.

SCENE THREE

A bedroom. Night. Ken punches a punchbag in his pyjamas. He really goes for the bag.

Ken Self . . . regulate . . . Self . . . regulate . . . You are strong. The world is . . . the world. Calm. Calm. You are so calm. You're motherfucking uber cool so fucking uber calm, Kenneth Tyrone James. Calm.

He breathes into a paper bag as he can feel a panic attack coming on.
A cinefilm of his kids playing shows. Ken and his kids. Running around. Happy.

SCENE FOUR

A law centre. Laura sits at a desk. Shaun sits opposite her. Reading a book. He wears an iPod. Moves a little with it. Laura types fast on her laptop. Shaun stares at how fast Laura is typing. She catches Shaun's eye. He shouts, unaware of shouting.

Shaun You're very fast.

Laura nods. Shaun takes out his earphones.

I bet you wish you could just stop all of that, don't you? The machine . . . Do you sleep here sometimes, do you? When you work late.

Shaun indicates the yoga mat behind Laura.

Laura It's a yoga mat.

Shaun Bikram is it? Or Dru or Hatha?

Laura Hatha. And sometimes Bikram. In the winter.

Shaun Heat in the winter of course. It makes sense. Are you really typing words there or just pretending?

Laura I did the Pitman course.

Shaun (*indicates his book*) *Disgrace* it's called. Very good. South Africa. Students and sex and shame. The man has been so bad he buries dead dogs in plastic bags to redeem himself.

Laura How long are you going to wait? Gail might be hours.

Shaun 'Love all, trust few, do wrong to no one.' Shakespeare.

Laura Right. But you understood what I said? We can't help you. The best number is on the back there.

Shaun I was here before. Gail helped me.

Laura I told you, it's changed. Since LASPO.

Shaun I don't like acronyms. They generally have something to hide.

Laura Why don't you come back later then? Before we close?

Shaun I am an associate of Gail's. I'm not a stalker. Or a hanger-on. Am I bothering you, young lady?

Laura No.

Shaun Good. It's better than the doctor's. It's quiet.

Laura Not on a Thursday.

Shaun And you don't get a ticket here. Over there it's like you're a leg of ham at the supermarket. Last time I was number fifty-nine.

Laura The Citizens Advice Bureau is on the map on the back of that. It's three short bus rides.

Shaun I've no Oyster card. What is your name?

Laura Laura.

Shaun Laura . . . Petrarch's doll. Maybe you'll lead me through the limbo of the housing system? By the hand? Laura . . . what is your definition of public transport?

Laura Bus . . . tube . . .

Shaun Transportation for the general public, no? I refuse to get on to erroneously named public transport for which you cannot give legal tender. Which is money. Or stamps even. This country, it is all about the paying customer now not the citizen. They used to call us passengers on trains, now it's customers. Vile. I tell you something, Laura, I refuse to be a slave to the Oyster. And don't ask me about my Freedom Pass. I have lost more of them than I have had hot dinners. It's a piss-poor vision of freedom, isn't it? A free ride to another bus stop next to some godforsaken bus shelter.

Laura How do you get around then?

Shaun I walk. I thumb a lift.

Laura You hitch? In London?

Shaun I mostly walk, true. With my thumb out. But it's the principle, Laura. My friend is dying though. And he's leaving me his car.

Laura That's nice . . . that he's leaving you his car.

Shaun Yes. But we can't be certain when he'll die. It's been a few years now.

Laura But he's ill.

Shaun Oh no, that Phelim's an awful liar. He is ill. He must be, the colour of him. Though sometimes I wonder if the Ford Escort is simply a way of getting drinks out of me. 'You're having my car, Shaun! When I go,' he says. As soon as he walks into the pub. Every time. Can I show you these letters at least? How is Gail? Did she ever find a chap?

Laura No.

Shaun We talked rent caps for hour upon hour. It was a complex case. I had a landlord who made Moriarty seem affable. What a waste of precious time.

Laura You lost the case?

Shaun We were triumphant. But to be talking rebates with such a lovely young woman. We could have been dancing. Or drinking cock-a-tails.

Laura Right.

Shaun In my time, Laura. When I was young. I was a wolf. Beware.

Laura Right.

Shaun I grew up very quickly. I loved horses as a lad. And books. I ate them up. Anything. Dick Francis, Jack London. Hated school. Except for the one occasion when I found an edition of *Fiesta* in the school playground. A sweaty pubescent kid I was.

Laura I'm really sorry, Mr Kennedy, I've got to make some calls.

Shaun Shaun . . . So there I was staring down at this well-thumbed magazine. Such vivid and varied shades of pink against the cut green grass. I claimed it and stood behind a shed and read a story of this woman who was all in her riding gear – hats, boots, jodhpurs – and she had lost her horse. Then she happened upon a barn. And it was a very hot day. And she progressively took off all her clothes. The horse never appeared . . . But this forlorn rider she had the best of times in the barn. By herself, mind.

Laura Okay.

Shaun And I still see her. Long dark hair. Hay rick. Eyes closed.

Laura Shaun . . . You're not facing imminent eviction. We can't help in cases like yours.

Shaun Imminent. Yes. You said. You've covered your back for when the boss gets back. It's just these . . . letters.

Laura Let me see them then.

Shaun I'll wait for Gail.

Laura Or come back on a Thursday. When we have our drop-in clinic.

Shaun I've no disease. And I've walked four miles to get here, Laura. Don't worry about me. I am invisible.

Laura starts to type emails again and concentrate on her computer.

It's a super power, isn't it? As a kid you'd do anything for a cape of invisibility. But as you get older . . . Wordsworth, he described his first night in London and he saw *Jack the Giant Killer* on stage. And the Giant wore a huge notice saying 'Invisible'. And the Giant was huge but everyone accepted that he wasn't really there. I feel like that . . . sat outside the job centre. On a bench. That there is this ferment of emotion. But no one sees it.

Laura keeps typing. Shaun reads his book. Then he looks to Laura.

I did have a girlfriend in the last few years. Venezuelan she was. Beautiful woman. Some of my sweetest moments were lying in a square in Euston with her and staring up at the trees. No words. No touch. Just us and the leaves above.

Laura gives up and looks over to Shaun.

But she was deaf. It was difficult. I shouted sweet nothings to her in bed. It's not love's young dream, is it? Stone deaf.

Laura Profoundly deaf.

Gail enters.

Gail Well that was a farce. Kalina turned up without her passport and paperwork. So we had to make another date.

Laura Did she forget them? She seemed really sorted.

Gail I think her parents told her not to bring them. I think they think it's all going to be confiscated or something. There was a cock-up and no translator. It was ridiculous. Oh hello . . . How are you?

Shaun Gail. You remember me? Shaun?

Gail Of course, Shaun. How are you?

Shaun I'm sorry that I only turn up here in times of need, Gail.

Gail That's okay. That's why we're here. What's the problem?

Shaun I've these letters.

Gail Shaun's last flat wasn't fit for rats. The new place is good though, isn't it?

Shaun It's perfect. I wake up every morning there feeling blessed. But they gave me an overpayment. I didn't realise . . . and I've no money to pay it back. I'm worried they'll stop my housing benefit now.

Laura I gave him the CAB address.

Shaun Don't give me acronyms. Two years ago you saved my life. She saved my life, Laura. I'm asthmatic, you know. I'd have fucking died in there. Taken my last breath staring at a wall of mould. But Joan of Arc here, she waved the flag at the fat man and he had to give me back my deposit and he made reparation. I've never had reparation in my life. Fucking heroic she is.

Laura She is.

Gail There've been huge cuts, Shaun. We can't help unless you're about to be homeless.

Shaun Can you at least read the letters?

He gives Gail the letters.

Gail How's Mr Ergen?

Laura He won't give up his dog. He says he'd rather die than give Harold up.

Gail He's got a fortnight to get rid of him.

Laura He says he won't. That they'll live on the streets. He brought Harold in here earlier . . . It's Mr Ergen's eightieth birthday tomorrow.

Gail I thought it smelt a bit dog. Dog and bleach.

Laura Harold's very old. I had to clean the floor.

Gail He peed?

Laura Spittle.

Gail reads Shaun's post. There are three standard letters.

Shaun They overpaid me. Their mistake. Do you see?

Gail You're going to have to pay it back. In instalments.

Shaun I don't have it. I rang them but they're all machines. I wrote to them but then the second letter came. I went to see them and explained that I've nothing and then a third letter came.

Gail They won't do anything for a while. You don't have any money, Shaun? Savings?

Shaun No.

Gail And they want five hundred pounds.

Shaun Five hundred and seventy three.

Gail Can you borrow a hundred just to keep them quiet?

Shaun No.

Gail Fifty? Anything?

Shaun I've nothing at the moment, Gail. I was waiting on a couple of jobs but they never got back to me. Suffice to say no one is head-hunting me. And myself at the prime of my life, eh, Laura?

Gail Okay. Well, you've got to go back then, Shaun. Tell them you're facing hardship and that they need to rethink your case.

Shaun Will you ring them?

Laura We can't.

Gail We can't make any exceptions.

Shaun Right . . . Thank you, Gail. Laura . . . it was a pleasure.

Laura Shaun . . . Do you want my Oyster card? To get back?

Shaun I don't touch them. Thank you though. Walking is very good for you. Your health. The depression factor. Also it is meditative. Some people they walk to Istanbul.

Laura It was nice to meet you, Shaun.

Shaun A pleasure. Gail.

Gail Goodbye, Shaun. Pop back in. Give us an update. If the Citizens Advice can't help then do ring us, okay? But they'll be able to help sort it.

Shaun leaves.

Laura He was here for an hour.

Gail He looks different. Much older. He used to bring me huge bunches of wildflowers and pampas grasses that he picked from the marshes.

Laura Sweet.

Gail He was a sailor most of his life. His mother was ill and he was looking after her. His daughter was a bitch. Greedy. Did you get round to the accounts?

Laura I've done a rough spreadsheet. It's not great. We're down by about three thousand.

Gail But we're owed four and a half.

Laura I've factored that in.

Gail We're still down three after we receive the four? No, that can't be right.

Laura I'm going to be paying the rates bill. Then we're two thousand nine hundred down.

Gail I'll have to ring Taylors and Burn.

Laura We haven't got time for interns.

Gail We'll make time. For a few weeks or months.

Laura How much are they giving us?

Gail Just a few hundred for training them up.

Laura Okay . . . Well, they might be great.

Gail No matter if they're not. At least they're still interested in this side of it.

Laura How was the date?

Gail Useless. Embarrassing.

Shaun walks back in.

Shaun I forgot to tell you something, Gail.

Gail Right.

Shaun Those buses. Do you remember they wouldn't let me get on with a can of Dulux? When I was trying to cheer up the House of Usher with a lick of paint?

Gail Yes. Bastards.

Shaun They're not consistent either. Livestock for instance. You can take pigeons on the bus. I have. Often. But not bats or snakes. In cages obviously. I'm not saying let them slither around the luggage bit or flap around upstairs. I gave my pigeons away. It wasn't fair on them, you know? They need to fly and I hadn't the time.

Gail Did you need to tell me something, Shaun?

Shaun Oh yes. I have become persona non grata at my doctor's. I shouted about an increased dose of morphine for my mother. She was in so much pain. And today. I did have a drink before I got here.

Gail That's all right. I'm not your mother.

Shaun No. No, you're not.

Gail How is your mother ? Did she reconcile to your South American girlfriend?

Shaun And the receptionist there. No interest in anything except to hamper my efforts. She said I was aggressive because I asked her for her name. I was simply trying to establish human contact. I asked you your name earlier, didn't I, Laura? Did you think I was going to mug you?

Laura No.

Shaun Exactly. This receptionist was so fragile . . . Although obese, I must say. But so threatened.

Gail Perhaps you were being a bit emphatic?

Shaun And she is trained supposedly to deal with people in stressful situations and she herself, she needed treatment. Not to mention the weight on her.

Gail Okay. Is that what you wanted to tell me?

Shaun No. My mother died.

Gail Oh Shaun, I'm so sorry.

Shaun Yes. Three weeks ago. I don't seem to be coping too well.

Gail Just . . . go gently with yourself.

Shaun How does one do that? She died at home at least.

Gail Good. Your mother would have appreciated how you kept her in her own home and didn't cart her off somewhere.

Shaun Do you think? It wasn't much of a flat.

Gail It was hers. And you made sure she stayed there.

Shaun I didn't clean as well as she'd have wanted me to.

Gail I'm sure you did brilliantly.

Shaun No. I have these images of her, Gail. Towards the end. They won't go away. I think that might be what brings me down a lot. People should really die before they get to that stage. But she clung on. For what I don't really know. Maybe just fear . . . But death couldn't be worse than living like that, could it? Curling up like a baby animal? Yellow? Starving? Screaming.

Laura Do you want a cup of tea, Shaun?

Shaun No. Do you have a sherry?

Laura reaches under her desk and produces three glasses and a bottle of fine sherry on a tray. She pours a drink for each of them and they clink glasses and drink. Shaun is happy, they do a little music-hall type dance move or two together, they laugh. Then Laura takes their glasses and restores the tray to its cubby hole. They resume normality.

Shaun She worked very hard for us all. I remember one time when we were dead broke and I was a boy and I heard her and her friend Minty talking about them becoming prostitutes. God they laughed. 'Who would have us?' my mother said. And Minty – who had no front teeth and a funny eye . . . They were on the floor in stitches. But the discussion had started out as a serious option. In hushed tones. I hope that she knew that I loved her. That's all.

Gail She would have known that.

Shaun I've not known real grief before. My father . . . nothing. But now . . . there's a calm to it. Sort of beatific. But I can't seem to do the ordinary things.

Gail You'll come through. And get things done. Just take things slowly.

Shaun I can't. This is an ultimatum. I explained to the girl at the council that I was in mourning. She just repeated the questions a bit louder.

Gail Go to the Citizens Advice Bureau. They'll get someone on it.

Shaun Death is expensive too, isn't it? The salesmen . . .

the fuckers are on to you with the flowers and the 'We're going to do something that would make Mum really proud.' I said to them 'I never called her Mum. And fuck off.' She wouldn't have wanted all that chrysanthemum yellow and white crap.

I got drunk at the funeral and I kept buying rounds. They never came to visit her but fuck, they could drink all right at her wake.

He gets out some cigarettes.

Gail Let's have a cigarette outside.

Shaun Sorry to burden you.

Gail It's not a burden.

Shaun What shall I do about these letters?

Gail I'll ring someone at the CAB. Tell them to expect you.

Shaun When I was growing up the poor were seen as unfortunates. Now they're seen as manipulative. Grasping. Scroungers. It's very sad.

Gail It is.

Shaun Society has always been divided. But in the past it was about giving alms to the poor. Now it's about kicking a dog when he's down. As though one were destitute through malice you know? Not circumstance or just a disinterest in money.

Gail We'll get you some advice. Clear it up.

Shaun You'll deal with it?

Gail We'll find out who's best for you to talk to there.

Shaun Thank you, Gail. That means a lot to me. I've this strange thing – never had it before – I want to hold people at the moment. Like life rafts. I keep seeing people and wondering if they'd mind if I just held them for a few moments. Almost for breath. Can I hold you, Gail?

Shaun holds Gail. Laura looks back to her emails. He holds Gail for some moments. Then they go out to have a cigarette.

SCENE FIVE

Ken and Gail dance together close and slow. Riz and Aisha stand beside each other; they put garlands of flowers around each other's necks. Then they kiss. They keep in motion in muted light. Shaun dances to the music of his iPod.

A bedroom. Day. Gail is in her underwear, getting dressed. Ken sits on a chair, half dressed.

Ken I have to be able to self-regulate.

Gail What?

Ken I have to be able to control my emotions in court surroundings . . . What was the technical term? For me?

Gail A litigant in person. They're generally dreaded. They don't know what they're doing and they waste a lot of court time so if you can navigate it and make the right points that will really impress the judge. Are you going to get dressed?

Ken How many people who represent themselves succeed?

Gail No idea. Some judges walk out because it becomes such a farce.

Ken It'll be fine. How hard can it be to say you want to see your kids?

Gail They'll get quite stuck on the fact that you haven't gone for mediation.

Ken I told you. I'd go. But Ellie won't. She's already got a solicitor.

Gail And you absolutely can't afford one?

Ken No. It'll be fine. You've got a lovely shaped back.

Gail Ta. Have you ever been to court?

Ken No.

Gail You should probably go along beforehand. Watch some cases. So you'll be less thrown.

Ken I won't be thrown. Can you not go in late today?

Gail No. I have to see a man about a dog . . . seriously. A pensioner who'll be evicted if he doesn't give up or destroy his dog.

Ken You could come to court with me.

Gail I really couldn't . . .

Ken Are you okay?

Gail Yes I'm fine. You?

Ken I feel good. It was a good night. I like your place.

Gail It's chaos.

Ken It's nice. We should meet again.

Gail It's going to be hard . . . to remain calm, standing opposite your wife who has been denying you access.

Ken Ex-wife.

Gail You're still married.

Ken Ellie's living with someone else.

Gail We just slept together. But you're still married.

Ken I'm separated. Sorry. This isn't very . . .

Gail What? The sex was good. That's done.

Ken Oh. Okay. So do you want to meet on Saturday maybe?

Gail I don't know.

Ken Why don't you know?

Gail They may throw some vile stuff at you in court.

She puts on her make-up.

Ken I've done nothing wrong . . . You're very good. At compartmentalising.

Gail Am I?

Ken We were making love together an hour ago.

Gail You've got a nice body. Subject closed.

Ken So have you.

Gail So what time you're on will be important. An early slot is best. Your hearing might be more informal. Around a table. Or more like high court.
You can take someone you know in with you to take notes. Who do you have?

Ken No one like that . . . Fuck. I just want to see my children. It's the most ordinary thing in the world, isn't it?

Gail You can go out and buy a Spiderman suit and some long rope . . . or you can do this with me, Ken. Why does your wife hate you so much?

Ken Because I had the affair.

Gail And that was the only one?

Ken Yes. Plus a one-night stand. Which she doesn't know about.

Gail Okay.

Ken Ellie wasn't interested in me any more. Only the kids. I saw Molly for a few weeks. That doesn't mean I should be prohibited from seeing my children.

Gail Where did you find Molly?

Ken I didn't 'find' her. She was an intern at the company.

Gail Great.

Ken But she wasn't young. She was twenty-five.

Gail Right.

Ken I did everything for Ellie. All my decisions were for her. Everything was for her.

Gail Even shagging the intern. That was a real sacrifice you made for her, Ken.

Ken Don't do that. Fuck this.

Gail I've really got to go soon.

Ken I was unfaithful because I became completely invisible to Ellie.

Gail Facts are what they want. They'll probably ask if you ever hit your wife?

Ken Ex-wife. No. I didn't. Never.

Gail 'Were you ever violent towards your children?'

Ken No. No!

Gail 'Did you ever threaten violence towards them?'

Ken No.

Gail 'Were you ever overtly sexual towards any of your children?'

Ken Leave it now . . . These are my children we're talking about.

Gail 'Did you ever abuse your children?'

Ken No. Fuck it. Don't . . .

Gail 'Did you ever shout at them?'

Ken Yes, I have shouted at my kids. Yes! Shoot me.

Gail 'On a daily basis?'

Ken No.

Gail 'And you were unfaithful to your wife? Several times. Over the period of a few weeks? You were having intercourse with someone else?'

Ken It was a few months in fact.

Gail 'And was this lover over the age of consent?'

Ken I'm not even going to answer that.

Gail I wasn't seeing a huge amount of self-regulating there, Ken.

Ken We're not in court.

Gail It's going to be harder in court. With your wife staring at you, next to her solicitor who's been trained to pummel you.

Ken I'll be contained.

Gail You'll feel rage and shame in equal and vast measures. You'd better concentrate on some anger management before your court date.

Gail stares at Ken, he at her. The anger translates to tenderness and she touches his face and he touches parts of her body. She hums to him. Tender. It is beautiful and sensual. Then they resume normality.

Ken I had a fling while my wife was treating me like shit. In France they wouldn't bat an eyelid about that.

Gail Are we in France?

Ken No.

Gail No. We're not. This is Uxbridge, not Paris. And you're fucked if you can't control yourself. It's evident you can't control your cock too well. Nor your temper. You'll have to tone up and find some inner strength somewhere. From your children. Or your faith. Or a self-help book. Or Valium.

Ken I have inner strength. And I'd like you to stop talking about my children now.

Gail Why?

Ken Just . . . stop. Okay?

Gail This isn't normal life now, Ken. You're in the System. Do you realise how terrifying that is? They can prevent you from seeing your children.

Ken Let's stop now.

Gail For ever. Just because they don't like the look and sound of you. And then what do you have? A garage full of catheters.

Ken You're . . . strange.

Gail I probably am, yes.

Ken You're fucking cold.

Gail is upset and cannot reply for a few moments.

Gail . . . Actually I'm not. And you weren't so great last night. It was a bit formulaic.

Ken Maybe because you looked better with your clothes on.

Gail Right. Goodbye, Ken.

Ken I didn't mean that. I'm not myself. I'm sorry.

Gail Grace is something you're lacking. It's something that people don't necessarily need and at the same time it's essential. Akin to kindness really. When Rudolf Nureyev was pursued by the paparazzi he didn't punch them. You know what he did? Hundreds of cameramen baying for his blood around him. He walked up to one of them and smiled and winked at the photographer and then he breathed on his camera lens. Enough now. Get out and good luck.

Ken leaves.

SCENE SIX

The law centre. Day.

Laura types at her computer. She rings a number and waits.

Laura Hello? It's Laura Mendes from the Cromwell Law Centre . . . Hi . . . Is Meena there? . . . We had a message from her . . . About a young Sudanese woman? . . . Yes . . . Can you tell her we've got space this afternoon at four if they want to come around? . . . Sure . . . Do you know is it immigration or DV? . . . Domestic violence. Okay . . . And do you know if she has any children with her? . . . No . . . Good . . . Thanks, Hannah.

Gail enters as Laura is putting the phone down.

Gail Hi.

Laura Hi. Did you call Mr Ergen?

Gail Yes. He's immovable.

Laura When did you speak to him?

Gail Half an hour ago.

Laura That's insane. He was here this morning. I spent forty minutes explaining to him. He brought Harold in with him again. I've used half of my face wipes. And I'm surprised Harold has any hair at all, he moults so much.

Gail Harold.

Laura All of Mr Ergen's friends are too old to walk him. He's a hideous dog. Ancient. Terrible breath. And his wounded ear smells. And he shivers. And Mr Ergen is wasting our time basically. He thinks the landlord will relent and he won't. Are you okay?

Gail Yeah . . . Who was on the phone?

Laura Southall Black Sisters. They want you to go there. I need to find a hostel.

Gail Are the interns coming? They could make some calls about it.

Laura One's in tomorrow and one on Tuesday.

Gail Okay.

Laura I got you that Separated Dads information.

Gail Oh . . . Is there a strange smell in here?

Laura (*sniffing*) No . . . Dog maybe?

Gail No, not dog. Have you been drinking your concoctions?

Laura No. Only lemons with coconut sugar. An hour ago. Are you okay?

Gail Yes. Why? Do I not look okay?

She gets down lower and sniffs for the source of the smell. Laura dials a number.

Laura (*into phone*) Hello? . . . Yes. I was wondering if you had any spaces at the moment? One woman, no children . . . I'm from the Cromwell Law Centre . . . Yes, repeated domestic violence . . . No? Okay . . .

She gestures frustration at Gail.

Thanks very much.

She puts down the phone.

Why do they ask questions when they've got no rooms? Some people have no concept of time management.

Gail I'm going to get some strong coffee. Do you want one of your things?

Laura Fresh mint. From the Turkish place. Can you make sure they take the leaves out though? Wait for one minute for it to infuse.

Gail nods and leaves. Laura picks up the phone and dials.

(*Into phone.*) Yes. Hello? . . . I'm from the Cromwell Law Centre and I wondered if you had any spaces? One woman no children . . . Yes, I can hold . . .

Laura holds, and types while she waits. Ryan walks in with a takeaway fresh mint tea.

Ryan Hey.

Laura Hey, sweetie.

Ryan Tea, fresh mint.

Laura Thank you.

She is glad to see Ryan but gestures at her phone.

Ryan Put it on speaker.

Laura What if it's my lover?

Ryan I want to hear him.

Laura puts it on speaker. There is some bad pop music playing on it. Laura looks at the tea. The leaves have been left in.

Laura Leaves.

Ryan I forgot . . . Just . . . ignore them.

Laura nods and smiles. She can't ignore them.

Laura He's a policeman. Who likes eighties pop music.

Ryan Right. He's tough then?

Laura No, he's the good cop – sensitive . . . But yes he's pretty tough.

Ryan You'd make a great policewoman.

Laura No, I've the wrong shins. Don't stay. Gail's around. She just popped out.

Ryan I saw her.

Laura Did she see you?

Ryan No. Me being here makes you work faster if anything. You type fast to impress me.

Laura types fast.

Woman (*on speakerphone*) Hello? Who is this?

Laura switches the phone back to normal.

Laura Hello? Laura Mendes, Cromwell Law Centre. We're wondering if you have any spaces at the moment? . . . No . . . Thanks.

She puts the phone down. But continues to type.

Ryan So she's a woman?

Laura Yep.

Ryan There's an Ozu season at the Prince Charles. Do you want to come along tonight?

Laura I can't. I've got to prepare for this case.

Ryan Tomorrow then?

Laura I'm going to be reading all week. There's just masses of it.

Ryan You are entitled to a night off.

Laura I can't . . . What? What is it, Ry?

Ryan I've hardly seen you this week.

Laura I've slept next to you every night.

Ryan Bodies lying next to each other doesn't really count.

Laura stops typing.

Laura You make it sound like we're dead. I love sleeping next to you. It's the best part of my day.

Ryan Going to sleep. Next to me.

Laura Yes.

Ryan You've become a human machine. You know that.

Laura No, I haven't.

Ryan You said the longer you worked here the easier it would get.

Laura I thought it would. But it didn't.

Ryan I was looking at caravans on Gumtree.

Laura I can't rent one from there. It could be filthy, Ry. We'd spend all week just cleaning it.

Ryan They put up pictures.

Laura It's not necessarily an accurate representation?

Ryan We could go and see it.

Laura When? When do I have time to go and see it?

Ryan I just want to see the ocean. Get away from concrete.

Laura Go. Nobody's stopping you, hon.

Ryan With you.

Laura Summertime then. We'll do a long weekend. It'll be brilliant. Has Kahlo gone through the cat-flap yet?

Ryan He won't do it. He just sits next to the door waiting for me to open it.

Laura Don't open it. We have to train him.

Ryan We've been opening doors and windows for him for years. He's just perplexed.

Laura He'll do it. He has to become more independent.

Ryan You do realise he's a substitute child for us.

Laura No. He's a cat.

Ryan As long as we're faffing around with Kahlo you won't have a kid.

Laura Can we not talk about this here? Now.

Ryan You're never at home to talk to. Your skin is actually paler than when I first met you. Gail takes the piss.

Laura Don't say that in here.

Ryan Is it bugged?

Laura The cases take time.

Ryan I worked it out the other day – the hours, and what with all the pages they give you . . . you're actually on less than minimum wage.

Laura Don't do that. Don't work out my finances.

Ryan It's just not right. The hours you put in.

Laura So what should I do? Read less? Not pick up on a detail on page . . . twenty-seven, which could mean a sixteen-year-old can stay here and have an education rather than be shipped back to where his family is being persecuted? This is a real person. Not a Japanese auteur.

Ryan Ozu is real life. Kurosawa is more real than real life . . . You looked gorgeous this morning. Asleep.

Laura Because I was mute?

Ryan You look gorgeous now. Especially your lower lip.

Laura Shut up.

Ryan Really?

He approaches Laura.

Laura Have you come to fix my computer?

Ryan I have. My van's outside.

Laura Wonderful. Do you have one of those belts and all the tools hang off of it?

Ryan I do.

Laura stands against the wall, Mexican music plays. He is her cowboy and they kiss passionately. Then stop.

Laura goes back to her typing. Ryan sits down and looks at a law magazine. Gail enters.

Gail Hello, Ryan. How are you? Busy?

Ryan I am, yeah.

Gail Good. Tea.

She puts tea next to Laura who sees the leaves.

Leaves, I know. But I didn't actually have time to wait for it to steep. You need a handmaiden or something.

Ryan Or just a spoon. Or a night off . . . I wanted to take Laura to the pictures tonight.

Gail The great thing about the pictures is that you can always go alone.

Ryan It's a communal activity. A ritual.

Gail How's the novel going?

Ryan It's a novella.

Gail Oh. Okay. What I'd love about writing a book is that you're the only one who can truly interrupt yourself, aren't you?

Ryan There are other distractions.

Gail Has your man got off his motorbike yet?

Ryan He gets off it a lot. He talks to people. He does ancient ceremonies. It's just an odyssey in that he travels miles on it. I'll see you later, Laura. Gail.

He leaves.

Laura You really don't like him.

Gail I've no problem with Ryan, it's only the way he elevates his work above yours that irritates me. As if any monkey can be a solicitor but only the true artist can sit down all day and write about Kawasakis on dust roads.

Laura He respects my work. He just gets frustrated.

Gail Because he needs supporting. He thought you'd be earning enough to keep you both and a few years in you're still on 25K a year.

Laura That says more about you and your . . . whatever the opposite of misogyny is, than about Ryan.

Gail There isn't a word for not liking men because the dictionaries were written by men.

Laura He doesn't care about money. He just wants to see me more.

Gail Well, here is not the place to visit you. He's in and out like a dog on heat. You're not a schoolgirl and this is not a bus stop.

Laura I'll tell him to stop coming in then. He only stays ten minutes. It cheers me up.

Gail My bad opinion of Ryan is based solely on what you've said about him. You said he never once asks about your work here. What you're actually doing and achieving.

Laura He doesn't. But I don't really need him to. And I don't ask him about his book that much.

Gail Why would you? A man gets on a motorbike and shags a lot.

Laura It's an Oedipal odyssey. In verse.

Gail Okay. A man shags a lot of women including his mother. Rhythmically. I don't see how it can be an odyssey and a novella.

Laura He read some of it to me. It's beautiful.

Gail Good. Shall we get back to work then?

Laura He just needs to get a job.

Gail As long as you top up his Oyster card for him and pay the rent he doesn't need to get a job.

Laura He does work sometimes. And I only topped up his Oyster when his bike broke. We're fine.

Gail and Laura check their emails and stare at their computers for some moments.

Gail I'm seeing a doctor next week.

Laura Why?

Gail It's a date. He reads Andrew Marvell and lives in Chester, hopefully in his own practice with roses around the door.

Laura You need a philanthropist, not a doctor. Someone who can inject some money into here. What does he look like?

Gail This is him. He put up a joke photo.

Laura Ping it to me.

Gail I might move to the countryside. Help him to heal people.

Laura You wouldn't.

She sees the photo.

This isn't him.

Gail It's Dr Kildare. Richard Chamberlain.

Laura He's not going to look like this, Gail.

Gail No. But I'm not superficial.

Laura You can't meet him unless he sends a real photo.

Gail Of course I can. I've trawled through the nice-looking ones and they were boring. He might be brilliant. I'll leave the city. The debris.

Laura No. You're an addict.

Gail Maybe. If any letters come addressed to me personally don't open them, okay?

Laura Okay. I never would. Personal letters.

Gail Not just personal. Official. Don't open anything official with my name on.

Laura Okay. Is everything all right?

Gail I don't know yet. I can't tell.

Laura and Gail look at each other for a moment then Laura goes back to typing. Gail opens all their mail and lets the surreal amount of letters and envelopes fall to the floor as she quickly checks them while Laura types.

SCENE SEVEN

A restaurant. Night.

Gail sits opposite Andy, sixty, a doctor from Birmingham.

Andy So . . . you're a solicitor.

Gail Yes.

Andy Dr Kildare. Did you use to watch him?

Gail Not hugely.

Andy Richard Chamberlain. A handsome man.

Gail . . .What's Chester like?

Andy It's very . . . Roman.

Gail Yes.

Andy A solicitor, that's a very fine profession. But it's getting harder. I know. The cuts.

The LASPO. I expect you drive them insane in court. With your feminine mystique. 'Guilty as charged, my lord.' That's what I'd say confronted with you.

It's terrifying, Gail. They're killing our system of justice. And Grayling. A joke. Wasn't he the first Minister of Justice to have no legal background whatsoever?

Gail And Gove's the same. They're as bad as each other. Gove pissed on education and now he'll do the same to justice.

Andy It's not nice.

Gail Gove's in favour of capital punishment, you know? And a new royal yacht.

Andy Never nice to hear ugly words from a pretty girl.

Gail Sorry?

Andy That they should push you to that. It's very sad.

Gail Yes . . . You're right, though. It's really crashing down. One law for the rich, another for the poor. If there's no access to justice for everyone then there's simply no justice.

Andy I didn't look at the menu. Did you?

Gail We're not eating.

Andy For the wines. And I like to know what a place serves. Even if I'm not partaking. Don't you? I like menus. Do you?

Gail They're . . . okay.

Andy I love them. A well-drafted menu can be a work of art. And the typos in Greek restaurants. Wonderful. Have you been to Greece?

Gail No. You?

Andy No. Italy?

Gail Yes. You?

Andy No. I've been to Spain. But not the usual hell holes. It's hot in here, isn't it?

Gail Is it?

Andy It is.

Gail Are you . . .

Andy What?

Gail Nothing.

Andy Nerves. I suffer from nerves terribly. Is it my neck? I blush with it. Forgive me. Also sometimes I say something and don't even mean to. I'm thinking it and it just comes out . . . Now tell me all . . .

Gail Okay. I do have to go at quarter to seven though, Andy. I'm seeing a play.

Andy Perhaps we can have dinner next time? So . . . I was reading about your LASPO, and how the H2 train will cost what was it, fifty billion? And the whole of the Legal Aid budget is two billion a year. So they're more concerned about a fast chuff-chuff than keeping our justice system intact. And your lovely self-employed.

Gail You're very well-informed.

Andy The truth? I wanted to be able to discuss your world with you . . . so I did prepare a little. Is that – what would they say? – desperate? No . . . I have a curious mind. That's allowed, isn't it?

Gail It is. I'm sorry . . . I've done no reading about the NHS.

Andy That's just as well. I won't have it spoken of. Nor the BMA. Hideous state of affairs. Let's forget about the whole pack of them. We're entitled to a night off, eh? . . . I'm in heaven right now, Gail. This is nice. isn't it? Twenty minutes ago we didn't know each other. I mean whatever happens . . . human contact is so welcome, isn't it? I'm not saying we'll get married but just . . . talking, ideas.

Gail Yeah.

Andy I sense I'm not your type. And that's fine. I'm not many people's type as it goes.

Gail Right.

Andy All I mean is let's turn down the pressure cooker, unplug the steamer . . . Let's stop thinking of it as a date and we can just have a nice chat.

Gail Okay.

Andy Good. You look more relaxed now.

Gail So what is happening with the NHS?

Andy I'm serious. I won't talk about the NHS or the BMA.

Gail Is it that bad?

Andy Shh . . .

He puts his finger to his lips.

Isn't that nice? Just to stop talking, just to stop everything for a while.

They stop for a moment or two.

Do you ever meditate, Gail?

Gail I don't . . . I should . . . You do?

Andy No.

Gail You said your surgery was in the countryside? That must be peaceful at least.

Andy My surgery is rural. But I never said I lived there. Another story. Another story. Another life . . . And what else? Tell me all about yourself. I've been really looking forward to tonight. I was bereft when you said you'd rather have a coffee than dinner, but there we are. Each to his own.

Gail You're a fan of Andrew Marvell?

Andy Not really. I've decided to tell you the truth, Gail. For the rest of my life. I've got a strong feeling about you and I don't want to muck it up. A lady friend advised me to put that poetry stuff in. And you seemed to like it so that was sage advice. I don't know a sonnet from a sonata. Kazuko said I should put yoga down too, but I thought that was pushing the envelope rather.

Everything stops for a moment or two, while Gail forces herself to ask another question.

Gail Do you enjoy medicine?

Andy I'm doing a few other things at the moment. Law is much more interesting than medicine. Because it's not my field. So the judges? They walked out. And poured on to the street. I saw the pictures on the internet. That's something I would have liked to have witnessed. That's historic. Were you there?

Gail I was.

Andy Now . . . enough of history. To the future . . . what are you looking for in a relationship, Gail?

Gail It was a lovely sight. To stand there. And to be in it together. Saying 'fuck you' to Grayling and his clan.

Andy puts his fingers to his lips and mouths the words 'Don't swear'. He gestures towards Gail's lips.

It was good . . . One fucking beautiful moment. Where we said 'fuck you' and your fucking Legal Aid Sentencing and Punishment of Offenders Act.

Andy puts his fingers to his lips, irritated.

Fuck you and your oppressive regime.

Andy You didn't answer my question, Gail. About what you're looking for.

Gail What I'm looking for? Probably someone who doesn't want to censor me. Someone who I feel completely myself with. Where I'm not trying to shoehorn my way into their idea of the little woman. Or even the very clever woman or the high-fucking-achieving woman.

Andy This propensity to swear. I feel it's a gauntlet, isn't it? Am I right?

Gail You said you were forty-five on your profile.

Andy Did I? It's not a crime is it? I find these sites are incredibly ageist.

Gail Then you should put your real age and be proud.

Andy Proud . . . Well. Yes. I suppose. But then I'd attract a lot of old women.

Gail I'd better go actually.

Andy Don't.

Gail It's just the buses, they crawl along at this time of day.

Andy Gail . . . Listen to me . . . I've been struck off the register. Through absolutely no fault of my own.

Gail Right. In relation to what?

Andy Three cases involving a trio of hysterical women. One would have been bad enough. But three. I have had bad luck. I always did. And my ex took me for everything I had. She was a junkie and I didn't realise it. Finally she took the surgery too.

Gail Right.

Andy What are you thinking? Right now. Don't process it, just say it.

Gail Shopping.

Andy Right.

Gail And my bathroom. That's quite strange, though, that you wouldn't know . . . about the drugs.

Andy Because I trust people. I always have. That's my problem.

Gail So now you live . . .?

Andy With my mother. In a bungalow in Mickle Trafford.

Gail Right.

Andy It's on the A56 . . . Sorry. No penthouse, no OBE, but I'm very good company. You look perturbed. You're a beautiful woman, Gail. Tell me what's troubling you. Tell me the truth. I'm being completely honest with you. From here on in. So what's up?

Gail Nothing.

Andy I'm not Christie. I'd be behind bars if I was Christie. What's the matter? Truly?

He looks at the menu.

I think we should have a proper drink. I think we deserve it. We'll go Dutch, will we? Traditional on a first date. House wine looks good. A half carafe?

Gail It has to be quite serious though, doesn't it? To be struck off?

Andy Are you calling me a criminal? Well, lock me up then. You go on robbing the country with your lawyer's fees and charging people a hundred quid a letter. You continue to be a legal parasite, Gail. You carry on with that and good luck to you in fleecing the nation. And me, I'll carry on with dispensing medication when the bastards at the BMA come to their senses. Whenever you want to get off your high horse we can order some wine. I'm thinking rosé. Mateus.

Gail gets up and starts to leave.

Do excuse me, Gail. Was I just a bit too honest for you?

Gail leaves.

SCENE EIGHT

London. A room. Night. Riz and Aisha sit opposite each other. Aisha sews a dress.

Aisha She won't let me go out.

Riz She does, Aisha. Don't exaggerate.

Aisha To do the shopping. She puts four pounds in my hand and she looks at me as though I'll run away with it.

Riz This all . . . takes time?

Aisha I need you to support me.

Riz I do.

Aisha Then why don't you tell her to stop knocking on our door at night? If she's not knocking I am dreaming that she is knocking and I wake up. I hardly sleep any more. People go mad without sleep, you know that?

Riz We'll have a child soon. This is good practice. You get no sleep with a child.

Aisha Then I want to sleep now whilst I am childless. I don't need to practise insomnia.

Riz She's just getting used to you. Mother's older. And lonely.

Aisha I know many people who are lonely. They don't haunt other people's lives.

Riz Please, Aisha. Show some respect.

Aisha I have done everything she asks of me, Riz. Everything. But I need to know that it will not always be like this.

Riz Else what?

Aisha I couldn't stand it.

Riz What would you do?

Aisha I just need to know it will not always be like . . . servitude.

Riz She is testing you a little, that's all. Making sure you are here for the right reasons.

Aisha To cook and clean?

Riz A wife does cook and clean.

Aisha And a wife has some privacy with her husband. And she makes friends in a foreign city. Or goes to the pictures. What do you think? Is that unacceptable?

Riz No. But just let this period burn itself out . . . Mother feels it too. She calls it a teething period.

Aisha I'm not a child. Nor are you.

Riz I'd like you to call her Mother.

Aisha I did. She looked at me as though I were dirt.

Riz Mother is shy, that's what you don't realise. You probably intimidate her. You have had more education.

Aisha I'd like more.

Riz And how will you study when you have a child?

Aisha She laughed at the presents I bought. She called them cheap. These past eight weeks seem like a year, you know?

Riz You said the presents were crazy yourself.

Aisha My family has no taste. I don't expect them to be mocked . . . Please, Riz, if you don't back me on this I shall think I'm going mad.

Riz She is my mother. I have to honour her.

Aisha And I am your wife.

Riz And I will try to be a good husband. Everything's in chaos right now. You know that. The taxis are going under. This place. Everyone's a bit edgy. But it will calm down. We have to see the bigger picture. We are in this for life.

Aisha We've only just got married. This is meant to be the easy part. Did you know it would be like this? She's taken my passport, Riz.

Riz She's looking after it.

Aisha I can look after it myself. Why are you all infantilising me?

Riz Her room is the most secure. You want it to be robbed? It makes sense to have all the documents and jewellery together. We're a family.

Aisha Then protect me. Please. I am being insulted.

Riz It's just about making allowances.

Aisha I have. I've never been disrespectful. I came here absolutely open. And it's like I'm in some weird fairy tale. With a witch in the woods.

Riz This doesn't suit you . . . being a bitch.

Aisha It doesn't suit me being a servant either. I haven't even seen outside of Southall yet.

Riz Did you come here to be my wife or a tourist?

Aisha Am I going mad? Maybe I am. Maybe I see the world completely differently to everyone else.

Riz You haven't said anything to your family?

Aisha Of course not.

She takes out a pack of cigarettes from her bag.

Riz What are you doing?

Aisha I'll smoke outside.

Riz You've never smoked.

Aisha I did. I gave up for our wedding.

Riz You never told me.

Aisha It's not relevant. I'm not a smoker any more.

Riz You lied to me.

Aisha My nerves are in bits. I just need a smoke. Okay?

Riz Did you use Mother's money? Have you been syphoning change from her?

Aisha What? No . . . Riz?

Riz Good. We'll go to Kew Gardens for your birthday.

Aisha Syphoning? I really don't like that.

Riz I don't like cigarettes.

Aisha You smoke like a chimney.

Riz I don't like you to smoke.

Aisha Fine. I just need this right now. And I'll keep a last one for an emergency. But because I want to give up, not because you tell me I look like a slut with a cigarette in my mouth.

Riz I didn't say that.

Aisha puts a cigarette in her mouth. Riz approaches her and she steps backwards and towards him; it is other and sensual.

Riz I saw you with flowers in your hair and henna on your hands and I wanted you so much.

Aisha You tasted of tobacco. Beautiful. And strong.

Then they come back to normality.

Riz We'll all be better once the business is steadier. I just need you to be strong right now.

Aisha I am strong. I'm just unhappy.

Riz I need you to help me.

Aisha All I do is help. You know what your mother told me? That I'm lucky. That another wife she knows is locked in most days and she has to ask for shampoo when she has a bath once a week? Her mother-in-law pours some shampoo into her hand. Your mother told me this as though I should feel blessed.

Riz It's a true story. They live streets away.

Aisha Then you should be telling the police about it. I'll tell the police about it.

Riz None of that now. They're a family. They have their own code.

Aisha Of slavery?

Riz Aisha . . . things will level out. I love you. It's just about acclimatising.

Aisha I don't understand. And I'm just . . . hurting.

Riz Please. I'll talk to her.

Aisha What will you say?

Riz I'll tell her to be gentler.

Aisha Are you scared of her, Riz?

Riz What? Of my own mother?

Aisha Are you?

Riz Why would you ask that?

Aisha It's a simple question. Some people are scared of their parents. It's a fact. Through no fault of the child.

Riz Are you scared of yours?

Aisha No. They drive me insane, but not one bone in my body has fear of them. You?

Riz I'm not scared. Of her or of him.

Aisha Your father's dead.

Riz Exactly. He doesn't scare me. Nor my mother.

Aisha Okay. Well . . . talk to her then.

Riz I just said I would, didn't I? What are you trying to do to me?

Aisha Nothing.

Riz Well, don't. Everyone has their limit. You can push me so far and then there is no give. Yes?

Aisha Okay.

Riz I have a position here too. I'm not just a go-between. Tell her this, do that. I am the man.

Aisha I know that. And I want to be a really good wife to you.

Riz Good. Because that's the first time I've heard you say that.

Aisha I thought you knew it. That I didn't need to voice it.

Riz Just . . . acclimatise, okay. I had to when I came here. So did Mother. We all have our turn.

Aisha Okay.

Riz Acclimatise. Challenges are what make us into the people we become. We rise to it or we fail. This will all pass.

He takes away Aisha's pack of cigarettes.

Aisha I promise not to syphon money off your mother's feeble shopping allowance too.

Riz I'm taking these for your own good.

Aisha I promise I'll be a good girl. And do everything that you say. I promise I will give up on the idea of freedom or happiness. And of being visible in this word.

Riz Aisha . . . don't . . .

Aisha I promise to accept your insults and indifference to me with quietude and I will make you dinner and wash your soiled underpants and be an angel of a wife.

Riz Shut up, you stupid bitch!

Aisha I promise to be beholden unto you body soul mind and if you still want to keep your huge collection of filthy magazines under the bed I won't question that either. Even though it occurs to me you might have thrown them out before my arrival.

Riz hits Aisha. She reels.

I promise.

Riz threatens her with his fist.

Hit me again. At least then I will know this is real. And not madness.

Riz leaves. Aisha cries.

SCENE NINE

Outside. Day. Shaun sits by himself with a cigarette and he vapes.

Shaun Kafka's beetle. Wakes up. Changed. Hated. Ends up dying of the rotten apples that are putrifying in his back. Apples that his family have thrown at him . . .

When Mammy died – after all of that commotion, I sat with her there . . . for hours. I postponed the call for the high-viz men to come and zip her up into a bag. All I could say was, 'It's all right . . . it's all right, Mam. You're all right now.' Death made everything seem holy – the stillness around her . . . the stained shirt she wore seemed like a relic . . .

Depression is classless. Hamlet, he was depressed . . . and a fucking prince.

I am like Hamlet except I have no girlfriend and no friends and no skull and no flute and no ship and no travelling players and no castle and I am fucking old. So not so very like him after all. A gun . . . from PJ down at The Feathers. I'll shoot the people in the council . . . A man needs a roof over his head. Or does he? Lear managed without. Although he ended up alone. And then dead.

SCENE TEN

A family court. Day.

Ken sits. He nods towards Ellie, whom we do not see. Ken stands.

Ken My Lord . . . I . . . I . . . Sir . . . I have heard the case for . . . I have heard . . . and listened to the . . . I did hear . . . I . . . I really did hear. And my reply . . .

He reaches for his notes. Starts to read them.

Glasses. I've left my glasses . . .

He holds the paper at arm's length and tries to read.

Ken looks at Ellie and sings, beautifully, simply, the Sanctus from the Missa Luba. He is open and bereft. Then comes back to normality.

Ken For five years I have been a father and a very happy and fulfilled father to my two children . . . My children are happy and well adjusted and I . . . My children, I haven't seen them for nine months now and that has been incredibly hard . . . I . . . My children . . . I . . .

He puts down the notes.

I have some notes to counter the remarks made about the last two years and I would like to refer to some articles in this text about . . . I . . . My children . . . I miss them. I miss my children. I miss my children.

He breaks down and starts to become angry.

You're killing me, Ellie! You're killing me!

He screams and then comes out of this anger. He is impotent now and can say very little.

SCENE ELEVEN

A bedroom. Night. Riz and Aisha stare at each other.

Riz I'm sorry. It's the job. It's everything . . . Aisha? I won't ever do that again.

Aisha You said that last time.

Riz And I meant it.

Aisha Riz . . .

Riz Aisha . . . I love you.

Aisha Riz . . .

Riz It was just everything – the tension. Mother on one side, you on the other.

Aisha I don't know what to do.

Riz It's going to be all right. Please . . . I didn't want to do that. It wasn't really me.

Aisha Every few days now.

Riz It was emotion. It was panic. I respect you completely.

Aisha I'm not scared of you. I refuse to be scared of you.

Riz I don't want you to be scared of me. I just need you to try harder.

Aisha No. I've tried. This isn't right.

Riz You're not scared of me. That's good. I don't want that. But you have to remember what everyone is going through. It's not just about you. I'm losing the firm. Most of the drivers I've had to lay off. They depended on me. That is a huge incentive for stress. It was my father's business. It was all that was left of him. He left it to me, Aisha.

Aisha Riz . . . you hit me.

Riz I didn't hit you. I push you. When you push me . . . to the limit. Most wives would be more supportive.

Aisha I just asked you what you were going to do? About the debts?

Riz And you think that helps? To be humiliated? And in front of her?

Aisha It was a question. A genuine question. I don't want to be here, Riz. And I can't go home.

Riz This is your home.

Aisha No, it's not. Nothing of here is me. Not one corner. Or window. Nothing. I only know everything through cleaning it. But not by sitting or being.

Riz Nothing has changed. The worst has happened now and we have come through it. It will get better from here on in. Now there is nothing to be scared of. I love you.

Aisha You hit me.

Riz Not hit. Push. Slap. Not hit, Aisha. Don't exaggerate. You keep thinking you can sort this mess out. You were doing my head in. Do you want a husband who is cold? Who does not care if you criticise him? I am your protector. But who is protecting me?

Aisha But I'm not harming you.

Riz Words are as harmful as blows. And before the words the looks. You take away my manhood. We are all three in the room together and you look at me as though I am shit on your shoe. Much as she does.

Aisha It's not meant to be like this. I can't do this. I can't do it.

Riz You're upset. Calm down. If we don't think calmly how can we find a solution?

Aisha What is the solution?

Riz Be less critical. Embrace the family.

Aisha I don't understand. I want my mum.

Riz Don't be a child. Your mother would say, anyway, you're a woman now, deal with this. See what he needs, your husband. See what his mother needs. Negotiate. Be wise. Your husband loves you so take the matter forward. Progress . . .

Aisha Do you love me though? Really?

Riz Why do you say such childish things? Aisha . . . Who else would I love?

Aisha But you're terrified of your mother. That's never going to change.

Riz That's not true. Take it back.

Aisha It is true. We can't go forward until you realise that. We can't be together until she's not in bed with us.

Riz No. You're speaking like some slut off the streets.

Aisha Am I? Perhaps I feel on the same level as them? Kicked by you. Spat at. Hit at.

Riz Don't . . . don't do this. Don't act as if you're some sort of martyr, Aisha.

We had a tussle. You provoked it. I forgive you, now please forgive me.

Aisha You don't even apologise.

Riz Life, Aisha, real life . . . it's a challenge. This is good for you. To see some real life. Let's start again. I'll start again . . . and you . . . you must let go of the resentment you bear towards my mother. Please. Try.

Aisha I have tried. Every day I try. She pulled my hair the other day and now it is coming out in clumps when I brush it.

Riz Try to put a good face on it. She won't always be here.

Aisha I'm not happy. I can't pretend to be happy.

Riz It was mild. Compared to what I used to get. Child's play. It did me no harm.

Aisha Perhaps.

Riz No harm at all.

Aisha Just admit that you're terrified of your mother. If you give me that truth I will try to make sense of it all.

Riz No.

Aisha You flinch when she says something to you.

Riz You're wrong, Aisha. You ask for it, you know?

Aisha I ask to be hit?

Riz I'm sorry. Sorry. Sorry! Fuck's sake sorry sorry sorry!

Aisha That's worse! Beat me then. Beat me on the bed. Come. I'll use the pillow to be quiet again.

Riz Don't . . . I don't mean to do it.

Aisha Beat me. Like you said. Let's look at the worst that can happen.

Riz takes off his belt and whips it into the air.

You beat me once more and I will go.

Riz Get into the bedroom. Your shouting will upset Mother.

Aisha You touch me . . . sleep with me . . . I will go.

Riz You don't tell me what to do.

Aisha I am going.

Riz You're not. You have nowhere to go.

Aisha I'll go to nowhere then. People do. They just get lost. I'll burn myself so people will know that something is wrong. They can't ignore me if I am blistered all over.

Riz And your family? When I tell them you have abandoned your duties as a wife?

I'll tell them you went off. Alone . . . or with someone. Both are shameful. Perhaps you have a lover? Perhaps I am being naive?

Aisha I speak to nobody. I wave at the woman in the nail salon. I go to Costcutter and the market once a day, where would I find a lover?

Riz You see . . . the word comes easy to you.

Aisha Do you see how monstrous this is? Against God? Against everything?

Riz I see you changing. And I am dying inside. That is all I see.

Aisha walks away and Riz follows her.

SCENE TWELVE

Outside. Day. Shaun drinks from a bottle of wine.

Shaun I'll drive to the woods and make a fire of all this council shite. And that way I will be cleansed. Those poor women. Who burn themselves. That one monk . . . such pain he must have been in, but still he sat there aflame and just gently keeled over. My face is hot and my feet are frozen. I'm nine years old. There's a humped bridge with wide steps over the canal. The river would always freeze over. And on to the tarmac surface of the bridge we have thrown more water so there is a solid frozen slope, We each sit on a kitchen tray and career down the slope. 'This is it!' the speed of it. The danger.

'This is real life!' I am ecstatic . . . Maybe killing the bureaucrats would give me the same sort of euphoria. PJ owes me a favour . . . he'll get me a gun.

SCENE THIRTEEN

The Southall Black Sisters' Centre. A room. Day. Aisha sits on a chair.

Aisha I was walking through the High Street and it was sunny for the first time. I was about to buy the potatoes. And I suddenly thought I don't want to carry all that weight if I'm going across town. Although I hadn't planned to go anywhere. I saw a cigarette on the road. Untouched. And I picked it up and asked an old man for a light. And I asked him if he'd ever been to the police station and he said, 'No, not around here.' He'd been once to Bayswater. I sat on a bench in the sun and smoked my cigarette like treasure. It was so beautiful. Sunshine. Sparrows. So simple. I tried to get on a bus but I needed a card. And four pounds wasn't enough for it in the shop. I started to cry. The woman from the nail salon saw me. She came out and I think she put her arm on my shoulder. She gave me her Oyster card. I needed three buses. The ride there was strange. Heightened. The river, the trees, they were so beautiful. The houses huge. There was an interpreter at the police station who was about to leave. She was from Karachi. They asked her to stay and help to translate. I said there was no need but she smiled and sat down. They gave me a coffee. When I started giving my statement I felt so important. Listened to. It was real now. That I was being attacked by my husband. That he . . . that his mother hit me. The police, they listened and then they left the room for a while. The interpreter was friendly. Encouraging. She had nodded at my story as though she had heard it before. When we were alone she said to me, 'You have come here and now you know what you must do? You should go back to your husband and endure whatever is going on. You mustn't bring shame to your family.' Then she was quiet and looked back at her phone. The police came back in and said that they couldn't help me and that I should go home. And then they said they needed to keep my mobile. I had bought it cheap, a pay-as-you-go. They took it. And they saw me out the back door. By the dustbins. It smelt of blood and meat. Gone bad. I got the three buses back to Southall.

Gail approaches Aisha.

Gail Aisha? I'm Gail Shaunessy. From the Cromwell Law Centre. I hear you've been having a really difficult time?

Aisha Yes.

Gail I'm sorry. We've found you a room in a local women's hostel. Do you understand?

Aisha understands. Nods.

Do you have your passport at all?

Aisha No. No, I have nothing.

Gail That's all right. Most of the women here start out with nothing.
Aisha?

Aisha Yes.

Gail I've some horrible questions for you I'm afraid. Can you bear to answer them today? It just means we can make a start on a case for you.

Aisha Yes.

Gail Do you have anyone who we should call? Friends? Or family? In London?

Aisha No. Only Gita. I don't even know her second name.

Gail Gita. From the salon, yes.

Aisha What will happen? Do I have to go back?

Gail No. Absolutely not. We'll make sure you don't go back. And we'll protect you from your husband. All of these hostels are completely anonymous. We'll go through the different choices you have, if you're up to it?

Aisha Yes.

Gail There are systems in place to help you become independent. The first one deals with the initial three months. Okay? I have to ask you about the amounts of violence you've endured, Aisha? To secure a place at the hostel.

Aisha Yes . . . Sunday. We went to the Kew Gardens. Gita and me.

Gail It's beautiful, isn't it? You liked it.

Aisha I liked it. Very much. The trees they're amazing. You can walk up amongst the trees. You're as high as the trees.

Gail You are. I love those walkways. So, your husband, what sort of violence did he inflict? Did he ever knock you out?

Aisha takes out a small Tupperware box with some home-made cakes in it. She offers it to Gail, who takes a small piece and eats it.

Thank you.

Aisha It was my birthday. Sunday. What's your name? Sorry.

Gail Gail. Good. Good, that's a nice place to celebrate it. Happy birthday.

Aisha breaks down. Much of her fear and sadness comes out now.

Aisha I'm sorry, Gail. I'm sorry. I'm so sorry.

Gail Don't be.

Aisha But he forced me . . . He forced . . . into me . . . He forced me.

Gail That's all right. He won't force you again, Aisha. He won't force you again.

Gail takes Aisha's hand. Holds her hand tight. Aisha nods.

SCENE FOURTEEN

The law centre. Day.

Gail sits and types. Ken walks in with a large bunch of flowers.

Ken Hi.

Gail Hi. What are they?

Ken They're for you . . . Thank you. And I'm sorry.

Gail I don't want them. I don't really go in for all of that.

Ken Please. I'm sorry. How are you?

Gail Busy. You?

Ken Good.

Gail You got access?

Ken Not yet.

Gail I'm sorry.

Ken It'll be okay. I'm sorry that I involved you in all of that . . . I don't think I was quite thinking clearly.

Gail It's okay.

Ken Why don't you lock up shop for half an hour and have a coffee?

Gail Is it anything important?

Ken It depends how you qualify important.

Gail Okay . . . so if it's about both of us having a bit more time to say we're both okay I wouldn't say that's high priority.

Ken As opposed to what?

Gail I'm dealing with a woman who might be evicted because she can't pay the bedroom tax. She used to need both bedrooms in her flat. But her teenage daughter died. And now the government want her to pay tax on her dead daughter's room. And she can't afford to. So I'd probably best get on with that rather than try and understand you better over a coffee.

Ken What happens to people, Gail . . . it's not your fault.

Gail No. I know it's not my fault. But it's my job to try to sort it.

Ken Just be careful. Look after yourself. Don't become a martyr to the cause.

Gail What?

Ken Make sure you take some time out.

Gail And that's what we did, was it? Had some time out? Like in the middle of a boxing match?

Ken I was very stressed and for that I am sorry. Which is why I brought the flowers. You're very good women here.

Gail We're not good women. We're expert practitioners. We may not power-dress but we're not a knitting circle.

Ken I can't say anything right. I'll go.

Gail We have done some amazing law in this centre. One of the biggest cases about unfair dismissal was resolved here. It changed the law.

Ken Good. That's great. Gail, I just came to bring you some flowers. That's all.

Gail And you brought them.

Ken It does drive you insane. Not seeing your children. I am not myself.

Gail I know.

Ken Then can't you forgive me?

Gail I'm sorry. My partner here hasn't turned up. And I'm really behind.

Ken Okay. Call me if you change your mind. If you want a chat sometime.

Gail Okay. But I'm very busy. Generally.

Ken I know that. Wish me luck.

Gail I do. Of course I do.

Ken And I do you.

Gail Thanks.

Shaun walks in.

Shaun Gail.

Gail Hello, Shaun.

Ken I'll see you, Gail. You take care.

Gail I will. And you. Goodbye.

Ken leaves.

Shaun Gail. I need to tell you something.

Gail Go ahead.

Gail opens a letter. Rereads it and throws it at a bin. It misses.

Shaun Bad news?

Gail It's mostly bills.

Gail reads another. It really is bad news.

Shaun I'm going to the Council.

Gail What?

Shaun I need your blessing.

Gail rereads the letter.

Gail Shit . . . This is it. I need a cigarette.

Shaun I wanted to tell you something.

Gail Shaun, can you come in on the clinic day possibly? I need to follow up on this letter. Right now.

Shaun I need to speak to you, Gail. Please.

Gail And I'm saying no. I'm on my own. Laura should be here. She's late.

Shaun Your woman is on the corner. Having a domestic.

Gail Right. I've given you as much advice as I can give.

Shaun There's a limit, is there? No problem. That's all right. I'm all set.

Gail Good.

Shaun Goodbye, Gail.

He leaves. Gail rereads the letter. Laura storms in.

Laura He's insane. He's actually clinically insane.

Gail You've not been late in five years.

Laura I'm sorry! It was everything. Shaun just parted me and Ryan on the street. He said 'Dance with her. Dance. Don't shout at her. Dance with her.' And then Shaun took me in his arms and held me. Why did he do that?

She wants to cry.

Gail What's the matter?

Laura I can't do it any more. He just attacks my decisions. And Kahlo's disappeared. He finally raced out through the cat-flap yesterday morning with the shock of it all and he hasn't come back.

Gail Shock of what?

Laura Nothing.

Gail He'll be back.

Laura He won't. I thought it would be okay for a bit. And then the neighbours complained about the noise.

Gail You and Ryan? Were you arguing?

Laura The dog. Harold. Howling all night.

Gail What? What are you talking about?

Laura I agreed to be Harold's guardian.

Gail You've taken the dog? You hate dogs.

Laura Temporarily! Temporarily! That's what I told him! And he just says it's all about the job and never about him. And it's not . . . It's all about him.

Gail I don't understand. Why have you got the dog, Laura?

Laura Mr Ergen came round. He said he'd rather be homeless again. And all the time he was talking Harold was staring at me. Shivering. I said I'd take him while we sorted something.

Gail You can't do that.

Laura It was just the way he was looking at me.

Gail Mr Ergen?

Laura No. Harold. It's temporary!

Gail Laura . . . we've had a letter. We've got to move out.

Laura What?

Gail gives Laura the letter and she reads it.

Gail They've decided they can't let us stay here.

Laura They can't do that.

Gail They can. They have. We're always behind.

Laura They've never minded before . . .

She reads the end of the letter.

Tesco's?

Gail They want to make it into a local store. Actually there's nothing local and never will be about Tesco's. But they'll have offered them a vast amount.

Laura We'll find somewhere else.

Gail Not with the money that we bring in. It's impossible, Laura. And they'll be putting legal aid contracts out to tender in the future. The government will give the contract to the cheapest bidder. Tesco's says it might branch out into law.

Laura Nobody wants a supermarket representing them.

Gail People won't have a choice. They'll be told.

Laura It's impossible.

Gail They cut our budget by two-thirds. That should be impossible. But they did it. Why did you take that dog, Laura?

Laura If I didn't, who else would? He was just dribbling and sort of smiling . . . appealing to me. Shit. What does Tesco's know about the law? No. No, I refuse to leave here.

Gail I can't keep us on here.

Laura We will . . . we'll find somewhere else. They need us around here. They need real people. To listen to them.

Gail We'll go. And all the other small firms will go. Most of them have already. And people don't even know about it.

Laura Then we'll shout about it.

Gail We have been shouting. Nobody's heard.

Laura Seriously, what will we do?

Gail You can join a firm. I'll . . . move in with my doctor. You can have a baby.

Laura I don't want a baby. You have a baby.

Gail I don't want a baby either.

Laura I want my cat back. And for Harold to stop crying.

Gail He will.

Laura He did. As soon as Mr Ergen came round. I left them there together. That's why Ryan's gone a bit insane. Selfish. We can't leave, Gail.

Gail We've no choice.

Laura No. This is ours. Yours. But ours. We've . . . worked. I know every pattern on this wall. How to open the crazy door. The people who have been sat here. Thousands of people.

Gail I know. I'm sorry.

Laura No.

Gail We can't compete. We're small.

Laura We're not small. We're huge . . . Shaun said it was a good day to die. That's just his turn of phrase, isn't it?

Gail Yes. Nobody's going to die. Can you feel that? Underneath the floor?

Laura No.

Gail I feel like I've got jet lag. Shock, I suppose. Although it was always going to happen.

Laura We'll try and keep going.

Gail We'll try. Yes. That's as much as we can do. We'll leave when we have to. With our desks packed into boxes. On to the street. I saw a bag lady once get on to the bus with about twenty bags. The bus had to wait while she kept getting off to get more bags. She arranged them all very carefully and just stood with this wall of carrier bags filled with her life. A boy offered her a seat but she said no and just stood there next to her bags. There was a real dignity to it. Grace.

Slow and smoochy music plays, Aretha-type music. Gail approaches Laura and gives her the flowers. Laura throws them away and she and Gail dance, close, sad.

SCENE FIFTEEN

Outside. Day. Shaun stands and dances to his iPod. He stops and takes the earphones out.

Shaun The men came. Mild they were. Not thugs with baseball bats but holding clipboards processing the poor. Thank you, Phelim, for lending me your car. I was here once with my mam. A boy I was. Huge egg sandwiches we had that you couldn't get your mouth around. I played like a savage in the woods whilst Mammy smoked and stared at the stones in the quarry. We made a fire. Twigs and rubbish. And I shall make a fire today. Bodies on rocks in the ancient times. Eaten by huge birds or beasts, that was ecology. But I shall at least go quick. The smell of burning skin and petrol . . . No idea how long the pain. Only that it will take the weight away. I'm an animal who has no water. In the desert. Thy will be done, God. No. Mine. My will be done. A burning car is a beautiful full stop.

'And as he died
He looked bewildered
Like a child.'

I just want to be held for a moment. A touch. Before I go.

A searing bright yellow light.
Silence.
Then a blackout.

End.